PRAISE FOR OTHER BOOKS IN THE SERIES

"Contemplative and frank . . . A valuable read for those who have borne children, not just for those who haven't." —*Washington Post* (*Nobody's Mother*)

"A well-written meditation on not having children." —*The Malahat Review* (*Nobody's Father*)

"Each [story]—like life itself—is full of unexpected twists and surprises. But all of the narrators are honest, compassionate, and have something important to say." —*Toronto Star* (*Somebody's Child*)

"These are stories we must share, must acknowledge . . . This collection has the tenderness to find the beauty of your bleakest moments." —*Telegraph-Journal* (*How to Expect What You're Not Expecting*)

a family
by any
other name

EXPLORING QUEER RELATIONSHIPS

EDITED BY BRUCE GILLESPIE

TouchWood
Editions

TouchWood Editions
touchwoodeditions.com

LIBRARY AND ARCHIVES CANADA CATALOGUING IN PUBLICATION
A family by any other name : exploring queer
relationships / edited by Bruce Gillespie.

Issued in print and electronic formats.
ISBN 978-1-77151-054-7

1. Gays—Family relationships. 2. Gay couples. 3. Gay
parents. I. Gillespie, Bruce, 1975–, editor of compilation
I. Title.

HQ76.25.G54 2014   306.85086'64   C2013-906208-4

Proofreader: Heather Sangster, Strong Finish
Design: Pete Kohut
Cover image: abezikus, istockphoto.com

We gratefully acknowledge the financial support for our publishing activities
from the Government of Canada through the Canada Book Fund, Canada
Council for the Arts, and the province of British Columbia through the
British Columbia Arts Council and the Book Publishing Tax Credit.

MIX
Paper from
responsible sources
FSC
www.fsc.org   FSC® C016245

The interior pages of this book have been printed on 30% post-consumer
recycled paper, processed chlorine free, and printed with vegetable-based inks.

1 2 3 4 5 18 17 16 15 14

PRINTED IN CANADA

For our families

contents

Introduction

BRUCE GILLESPIE

JAPANESE PHOTOGRAPHER SHIZUKA YOKOMIZO takes a unique approach to finding subjects for her *Stranger* series of portraits. She selects an apartment building and then delivers anonymous notes to its residents advising them that she will arrive at a designated time one evening. If they are interested in taking part, they should stand in their front windows, dressed and posed as they see fit, with the blinds open and all available lights turned on, and she will photograph them from across the street.

I saw some of Yokomizo's portraits at the Museum of Contemporary Art in Chicago a couple of summers ago as part of an exhibit about skyscrapers and was struck by their honesty and the uneasy, almost voyeuristic tension they evoked between viewer and subject. As the exhibit's curators explained: "Empowering her subjects by inviting their participation, Yokomizo takes up the presumed privacy of the home and raises an awareness of exposure, certainly for those inhabitants who received her anonymous letter, as well as for the viewer. Out there, from the dark of the street, *they can see us*—whoever they are."†

The portraits stayed with me for some time, and I couldn't figure out why until I started to work on this book. That's when I recognized the similarities between our approaches. Like Yokomizo, as an editor of a collection of personal essays, I ask my contributors—some of whom are professional writers, some of whom are not—to draw back the curtain on their lives. I ask them to appear in an illuminated window on a dark night and provide us a glimpse into their homes.

It is no easy proposition to accept, to grant strangers such access and allow them to bear witness to some of the most intimate aspects of your relationships and family life, particularly if you're queer. (A quick word on language: I've been very thoughtful in choosing to use the collective noun *queer* to refer to lesbian, gay, bisexual, and transgender people in this book. Although it is a term with negative connotations historically that not everyone appreciates, many LGBT people have reclaimed it as a useful umbrella term for members of their community, as have I in this collection.) Until relatively recently, most queer people around the world had to keep their relationships secret or at least unspoken, both for their physical safety and in order to get along with straight society. But that has been slowly changing in the past thirty years, particularly in the Western world, as seen with the introduction of anti-discrimination laws and, more recently, same-sex marriage and adoption legislation. Although it may still irk people in some quarters, the idea that queer people have loving relationships that deserve the same recognition as their heterosexual counterparts is less and less a point of debate.

But the idea that those relationships may be understood as *families* is still contentious in many circles—including queer ones. For many queer people, the concept of "family" has been co-opted by the religious right, whose members preach that a true family may only consist of one man, one woman, and various children. Taken as such, the idea of family has been used to bash queer people and illegitimatize their relationships as something unnatural for a long time. For this reason, some queer people have a difficult time using the term *family* to describe the network of caring, mutually supportive, and loving relationships they create for themselves.

For others, though, reclaiming the concept of family is an act of empowerment that is at once personal and political. With such a seemingly small and insignificant choice of words, they affirm to themselves and the people and institutions around them that queer relationships can and should be understood as a type of family, even if we aren't used to calling them that. In doing so, they realize what adoptive families have always known—that the determination of who may be considered family is no mere biological matter. Nor is it something that can be decreed by others; as a friend of mine recently remarked, there's an important distinction between whom you're related to and whom you consider your family.

As the twenty-one essays in this collection illustrate, our relationships and families cover much of the same ground as straight ones—dating and first love, long-term relationships and parenting, separation and even death—but in a uniquely queer way. If there is one thing that queer people can contribute to our twenty-first-century understanding of what it means to be a family, maybe it's this: that it isn't one set thing. That a family can be many things and take many forms, some that may seem similar to straight relationships and others that push those boundaries but are families all the same.

So, come, step up to the window. We've turned on the lights and pulled back the curtains. Look inside and meet our families.

† Darling, Michael, and Joanna Szupinska, *Skyscraper: Art and Architecture Against Gravity* (Chicago, IL: Museum of Contemporary Art Chicago, 2012).

Rare Species

SARA GRAEFE

WHEN OUR SON WAS not quite three, he spotted his first glimpse
of a frog in its natural habitat, on the beach near my parents'
cottage in the Gatineaus. He was very excited—his only other
close encounter with an amphibian was in a tank at the Vancouver
Aquarium. I was excited too: it was the first frog any of us had
spotted on this beach, once densely populated with the little crit-
ters, for a long time. Back in the day, there'd be a series of splashes
the minute anyone set foot on the sand, as some dozen frogs bailed
into the lake. As a kid, I'd wake at night to the deep bass notes of
the bullfrogs' chorus. Just the sight of this tiny, speckled creature
bobbing in the weeds by the shore gave me hope—maybe the species was coming back. Maybe the local ecosystem wasn't going to
hell in a hand-basket as quickly as we'd all feared.

Our son, however, was more focused on the immediate details. "Where's the baby froggy now?" he wanted to know as I towelled him off after his swim, his gaze fixed on the spot under the neighbouring dock where the frog had hopped away moments earlier. A baby frog, in his toddler's eye view, because it was so small compared to the plump, animated bullfrogs he'd seen in books or on TV.

"Maybe he's still under that dock," I suggested.

"What's Froggy doing under da dock?"

"Maybe he's gone to bed," I hastily improvised, noting the sun slowly sinking behind the wooded hills at the far end of the lake. "It's night-nights time."

He nodded as he processed this information, so deep in thought that he didn't even remember to protest his looming bedtime. As I slipped on one of his shoes for the walk back up to the cottage, he asked, "Where's the baby froggy's mommy?"

I couldn't help but smile. "Oh, I bet she's under there too, snuggling him close," I imagined out loud, running with the bedtime metaphor. So what if I was totally anthropomorphizing the poor frog?

"What about his other mama?" he blurted out, concerned.

My heart swelled. Of course—why wouldn't the so-called baby frog have two moms, just like him?

"His other mom is cuddling him too," I reassured him as my wife arrived through the trees.

"Mama Manda!" he cried, running over and throwing his arms around his own "other mom." Amanda picked him up, meeting my eyes with a smile, obviously having overheard the last bit of our exchange.

She wasn't the only one. Over on the opposite neighbours' dock, two kids—about ten and thirteen years old—were watching the entire scene, transfixed. They'd been taking in their boating gear for the night but had stopped to gape at us. Clearly, they hadn't been exposed to a lot of queer families, at least not up close and personal on the lake. We were a novelty, a rare species like the frog, perhaps even a freak show—it's hard to tell exactly what they were thinking as they tried hard not to stare.

It's in moments like these that I'm reminded that being a queer parent puts me out there in the world in a much more visible way than I have ever experienced in twenty-some years as an out, proud, rainbow-flag-flying lesbian, be it as an individual or with a partner. I have no qualms about holding Amanda's hand in public, for instance, or kissing her goodbye on the sidewalk, but I also have street smarts—I can (and do) choose to forgo the kiss or drop her hand in potentially sketchy situations.

Being a parent, however, means being out there 24/7 as a queer family. In public, as in our son's private universe, I am without question his mommy, and Amanda his other mom, his mama. Neither of us is willing—or able—to disguise these roles momentarily, in the way that I might casually release Amanda's hand late at night as a group of drunken red-neck thugs approaches on the street. We don't ever want to cause our boy doubt or shame about who we are as his parents and about our place in society as a family. No doubt, he'll get plenty of those messages from other sources as he grows up. It's our job to foster his sense of confidence and self-worth so that he can deal with such messages down the road, and to model how we are a family just like any other—essentially, to just be ourselves.

⚘ ⚘ ⚘

I'm one of those women who's always known I wanted to be a mom. Not just any mom, but somebody's birth mom, an impulse that remained steadfast even after working for five years at a post-adoption support agency where I met some amazing, vibrant adoptive families. I chalk it up to biological imperative. All I know is, ever since I was a little girl playing with dolls, ever since I witnessed my mother's ballooning belly followed by my little brother arriving on the scene, I've had a deep-seated desire to experience pregnancy and bring my own baby into the world.

Coming out during my university years put a serious glitch in proceedings. This was the late 1980s / early 1990s, and the only dyke moms I knew were older lesbian couples who'd had kids in previous, straight relationships. I'd reached that point of no return where I could no longer keep hiding away in the closet, and one of the most painful aspects of my coming out was letting go of that image of myself as a mother. Wife and mother, actually, because I'd also grown up assuming that I'd get married one day—that's just what people did. The idea that same-sex unions could be legalized during my lifetime was unfathomable.

Oh, the tears I shed in my new buzz cut and Birkenstocks, as I found myself inexplicably flooded with grief as I kissed goodbye to some mainstream, hetero, white-picket-fence image of marriage and family, an image that had never really fit to begin with. Although I'd imagined myself as a mother ever since I was a little girl, there'd never been a guy as dad in the picture; I'd had crushes on other girls since kindergarten. And even though I self-identify as femme, on the three separate occasions in my twenties that I squeezed myself into a froufrou gown and sported a ridiculous up-do to serve in the bridal party of a straight girlfriend, I always felt as though I was in drag, a queer interloper in this exclusively hetero, age-old rite of passage.

A few years after graduation, I heard that an older lesbian I'd known back in my small university town—a therapist who'd supported me during my coming-out process—had just become a mom. Her partner had recently given birth to a baby girl, and they were fighting the Ontario government to get both mothers' names printed on the birth certificate. I was elated by the news of the birth, not only for my former therapist and her partner, but for me, baby dyke that I was. Motherhood *was* still possible.

By the time Amanda and I got together in 2004, same-sex marriage was newly legal in parts of Canada. It was the first time either of us had been with a partner when marriage was an actual option. I was thirty-four and my clock was seriously ticking. On our first date, pheromones and endorphins were already flying high when I spotted a pink, sparkly princess wand in the backseat of Amanda's car, not exactly in keeping with her butchy style. It turned out she was heading to her friend's afterward, to play fairy godmother at a three-year-old's birthday party. My heart skipped another beat—she liked kids. Within two and a half years, we were not only married but embarking on our own baby-making journey, suddenly weighing complex, life-altering decisions such as known versus anonymous donors, fresh versus frozen sperm, and DIY home-jobbies with a turkey baster versus pricey, highly medicalized procedures at a fertility clinic. After riding the highs and lows of the fertility rollercoaster for a short three cycles, I was pregnant. Our son was born in late 2007, smack dab in the middle of the current gayby boom.

We got our first taste of being "out" in the world as queer parents during my pregnancy. Amanda was helping me pick out my first set of maternity clothes, and the store clerk mistook her for my mother. Sure, Amanda is older than me — by a whopping eighteen months. There's no possible way she could be my mother, unless I was conceived while she was still in diapers. Amanda and I both froze, momentarily thrown, before I stammered, "You mean, my partner?"

This was our first inkling that as expectant queers, we'd entered a whole other world. We were gatecrashers into the hetero-normative zone of pregnancy, childbirth, and parenthood. Our maternity care providers were a pair of lesbian midwives, so we'd been sheltered from this reality for the first few months, until my growing belly started outing me as a mom-to-be and strangers scrambled to figure out where Amanda fit into the equation.

The maternity store incident proved to be the first of many such misunderstandings, which we've now come to accept as par for the course as a queer family. In public, we are either totally conspicuous, like that evening at the lake, or completely invisible. In the first week post-partum alone, when the three of us were confined to the hospital due to an unwanted C-section and breastfeeding difficulties, Amanda was alternately mistaken by nursing staff as my sister, my friend ("What kind of friend would put up with that crummy mattress on the floor?" Amanda wanted to know), and again, unbelievably, my mother. This, at the foremost maternity care facility in British Columbia, in a major urban centre boasting a large, visible queer population. On the flip side, there were nurses whose gaydar bleeped right away but who felt this somehow gave them license to ask a lot of prying, presumptuous questions: "So, is he a test-tube baby?" (Uh, no.)

There have been equally uncomfortable moments of confusion with the likes of customs officers, medical specialists, civil servants at BC Vital Statistics and Passport Canada, and even the locum filling in for our regular family doctor. "And who are you?" Amanda has been asked countless times, as though she's an afterthought, a hanger-on rather than a co-parent—often followed by a surprised, embarrassed "Oh!" as she identifies herself as our son's non-biological mother. Then there's the classic, "Who's the real mom?" To which we always respond, "We both are."

What matters most, of course, is that our young son has no doubt in his mind about who we are. Amanda is his mama, I'm his mommy, and together, the three of us—plus our two dogs, as he always reminds us—make a family. But what comes to matter more and more, as he grows older, is how he experiences being out in the world, as a boy with two moms.

On one hand, we share the concerns of any other parent whose child starts to venture into the world, solo, for the first

time. As our son transitioned into kindergarten, we found ourselves fretting: How will he cope all by himself? Will he make
friends? As queer parents, though, we always have that addi-
tional, niggling worry—how will our gentle, trusting, sensitive
boy make his own way in a world that doesn't always smile
kindly on families like ours?

"We are same-sex parents," we boldly declared in our ad for
a caregiver when I first returned to work, in order to avoid any
nasty surprises when we interviewed. "Applicant must be comfortable working in a household with two moms." But we can
only control the variables for so long. I dread the day our son
first faces a homophobic taunt on the playground or encoun-
ters an adult who casts aspersions on his family. Thankfully,
aside from a few forms where we've had to cross out "name
of father" and write in "name of mother" a second time, our
family's experiences to date with the school system have been
incredibly positive.

Nevertheless, our son's first forays into the world have
quickly shifted his perception of family. Now, at five, he wouldn't
necessarily jump to the conclusion that the "baby" frog at the
lake had two moms. Quite the opposite: he'd probably assume
that the frog had a mom and a dad, unless presented evidence
to the contrary. He's already grown to realize that his family
makeup isn't the norm.

When his class at preschool did a unit on the family, our
son, then three, proudly made a collage depicting his parents:
two women cut out of a clothing catalogue and pasted together,
the consummate dyke couple on green construction paper. But
he also started wondering about daddies. Up to this point, he'd

always substituted "Mama" for the father figures in picture books we read to him at bedtime. But now he was spotting daddies everywhere: "That's Henry's daddy," he'd announce whenever we revisited *The Potty Book for Boys.* "That's Trixie's daddy," he'd remind me as we worked our way through the Knuffle Bunny trilogy. "That's Christopher's daddy," he clarified as we laughed through Robert Munsch. "That's Jillian's daddy," he'd point out at preschool drop-off. "And Rose's daddy." On one occasion, adding, "I want a daddy too."

My heart sank. Here we go, I thought. His first sense of being *other.* And there's no avoiding it: there's a huge gap between seeing your family accepted and celebrated by the school and seeing your family reflected back at school as the norm. For several months, we watched him trying to figure out how the three of us fit into the images of family that he'd seen at school, images that he's bombarded with everywhere, every single day—pictures that don't quite match his reality.

"I have two teachers, two pugs, two moms!" he gleefully announced to me one day, as though all good things come in twos. Then quickly added, "And one daddy."

"Yes, you do," I affirmed, even though his declaration had caught me off guard. We hadn't yet had a conversation about the fact that he was conceived with the help of an anonymous sperm donor, someone who's open to contact once he turns eighteen. "And who's your daddy?" I asked, curious to know what was going on in his little head.

"Mama Manda!" he sang.

"So, Mama Manda is one of your two moms," I stated, struggling to clarify, "and a daddy?"

"Yes," he retorted, as though it were obvious. "A Mama Daddy."

I couldn't help but smile. We immediately recognized that Amanda's new designation was more about the role she plays in our family as the butchy "other mother" than about our son wishing she were an actual man and bona fide dad—although there have been hints of that since, particularly when our son was on the cusp of four, the developmental stage where kids want to identify with the same-gendered parent: "But, Mama, you are a boy, just like me!" he insisted on one memorable occasion, trying to drag Amanda into a men's washroom at Science World as strangers looked on, bewildered and amused.

When Amanda relayed the tale to another queer mom, a therapist whose two boys are now in their late teens, the woman shared an immediate laugh of recognition: her youngest went through the exact same thing with his non-bio mom at that age. She suspects a big part of it has do with our kids picking up on their other parent's butchiness and not knowing how to name or categorize it, rather than simply pining for a male role model or equating the parenting role of "other mother" with "daddy." These types of incidents have created important, teachable moments. After the washroom debacle, Amanda initiated a chat about tomboys. ("Mama, can I be a tomboy too?" our son wanted to know.)

"Yes, you do have a daddy," we explained to the three-year-old longing for a father. "A donor daddy." Our son took this all in stride. We were actively trying to conceive a second child at the time (albeit, unsuccessfully), and as a result our son, who had accompanied us to many medical appointments, had a fairly solid grasp of how he'd come into the world—he'd even made a painting in art class that he'd titled, *Mommy and Mama going to the hospital to make a baby.*

"What does he look like?" he wanted to know, so we showed him a glossy photo of his donor that had been provided by the sperm bank.

"Oh!" he said, entranced. "Can he come and play with me?"

"When you're older, you can write to him and ask."

This immediately seemed to satisfy his curiosity and quelled his daddy obsession for the time being. Now that we've introduced the notion of his "donor daddy," we don't hesitate to bring it up in regular conversation, if the situation warrants: "Yes, those boys are playing football. Did you know your Donor Daddy likes to play football?"

But last June, when his preschool teachers gently gave him the option to make a Father's Day craft for either his Donor Daddy or his grandfather, our son insisted instead on creating something for his beloved Mama Manda, even though he'd already presented her with a Mother's Day gift a month earlier. Her place in his life, and his four-year-old heart, couldn't be more clear.

Meanwhile, simply by being out in the world, our son has been a positive ambassador for queer families. If nothing else, he's already exposed his young peers to the notion of diversity. Product of my own generation, I didn't even know what the term *gay* meant until at least grade four, and even then, I had no context for it. Our son's preschool and kindergarten classmates, on the other hand, have already witnessed and embraced the idea that families come in all shapes, sizes, and colours. During that unit on the family at our son's preschool, our family photo was featured front and centre on a bristol board poster depicting the myriad families in the class. Recently, our son's new best friend in kindergarten went home and told his mother that he wished he had two moms too.

When I think back to that tranquil evening at the lake with my wife, our son, and the so-called baby frog, I wonder what the neighbours' kids saw as they stared at us across the water. I hope that, despite our differences and the apparent novelty of our queerness, they recognized a loving, nurturing family much like their own—one who, like theirs, loves the outdoors, after-dinner swims, and spotting rare frogs.

As I reflect, I'm reminded that it was on this very lake that I encountered my first lesbian couple, the first one I'd been consciously aware of, anyway—butchy, warm-hearted army dykes who'd bought the red cabin down the bay when I was about ten, the same age as the neighbours' son that night he stared at us from his dock. These outgoing women built a massive deck with a fire pit on the rocky ledge of their property, overlooking the lake. They held the most amazing parties there, with beer, songs, and laughter over the roaring campfire until the wee hours of the morning. They'd always smile and wave at me and my best friend as we wandered along the gravel road, their pickup kicking up dust as they passed. I remember being sad when they sold the place a few years later, a military posting taking them somewhere far away. They were so nice and, well, ordinary—they made being queer a possibility.

And now, as my wife, our son, and I continue to put ourselves out there in the world, day after day, as we go about our everyday lives, we are making family not only a possibility for the next generation of queers, but also a reality in the here and now, in a predominantly straight world that is still often caught off guard by our presence.

SARA GRAEFE is an award-winning playwright and screenwriter. Her writing about parenthood has appeared in *Literary Mama*, on the Momoir Project Blog, and at the Mamapalooza Festival in New York City. Her blog, Gay Girls Make Great Moms (queermommy.wordpress.com), chronicles her experiences as a queer mom in a straight world. She lives in Vancouver and teaches in the MFA Creative Writing Program at the University of British Columbia.

Requiem

KEPH SENETT

SOMETIME BEFORE I WAS born, my mother made a fabric art piece in remembrance of an aborted pregnancy. It was called "Requiem," a three-dimensional, stuffed silver vagina weeping a cascade of multi-hued satin tears. She built it a full four feet high and hung it in a hand-carved maple frame. My mother is not one to understate.

When I was a teenager, I'd horrify new boyfriends by inviting them home to see my mother's vagina. The thrill was heightened by the fact that the piece weighed easily twenty-five pounds and would unpredictably wrench its supporting nail out of the wall and crash onto my bed. I liked that it was shocking, but it was also a question asked of anyone I let into my room. *Would they understand my mother? Would they understand me?*

My mother was a preacher's kid, an only child who was moved from parish to parish throughout the southern United States with just her parents for company. When she finally got to college at seventeen—she'd worked desperately to skip a grade—she never looked back. It was the 1960s. She had sex, took drugs, got an abortion, enjoyed her first lesbian experience, raised her consciousness, and discovered feminism.

What my mother grew to understand with more clarity and anger than anyone I've ever known was that the simple accident of your sex at birth determines everything. As a girl, she was expected by her parents to grow up and marry. "They let me go to college for my BA," she told me once, "but only because they expected that I'd also get an M-R-S." But she refused to get married, and she refused to apologize for it. It was the same with her abortion. She grieved, of course, but hanging her sorrow on the wall was her way of honouring the life that wasn't, and it was her way of not apologizing for her choice.

When she became pregnant again, years later, she hoped for a girl. Of course, she knew she wasn't supposed to care, but she didn't apologize for her preference. When I was old enough to discuss it, she told me that she hadn't thought she'd know how to raise a boy and that she'd simply not wanted to try. In 1970, I was born—a girl—and from the beginning I knew two things: that my sex was significant and that I should never apologize. And if you're going to grow up to hang an enormous vagina on your wall, these are exactly the things your mother should teach you.

$$\mathfrak{L} \quad \mathfrak{L} \quad \mathfrak{L}$$

When asked to tell my coming-out story, I often say I was never really in. When I was five, my parents split up and my mother bought a renovated 1950s school bus that—geography be damned—she wanted to drive from Toronto to New Zealand. It broke down in the Kootenay Valley in British Columbia, so that's where I grew up, in the mountains. I was a hippie kid. I spent my childhood naked; I was free to be. There's an old picture of me running along the beach, my arms flung out from my body at the odd angles children achieve in their ecstatic states of play. The photo was used on a brochure for a 1975 conference entitled "The liberated child and the intimidated parent." Nobody, those unselfconscious arms said, was going to tell me how to find joy.

Later, I went to an alternative high school where, as in the "free schools" of my childhood, I was encouraged to participate equally in the institution's governance. In practical terms, this meant we called our teachers by their first names and got in less trouble for smoking than our peers at the straight schools. There were only thirty of us in my class, and we all paired off and broke each other's hearts and paired off again as regularly as any other teenagers. I quickly discovered that boys were far easier to bed than girls, so I had boyfriends. Sexual shame was low on my list of neuroses, but like all teenagers I harboured secrets. One of them was that I was constantly, painfully in love with my girl friends. All of them.

My eventual confession (in the mid-1980s, it was de rigueur to declare your homosexuality in the brave tone usually reserved for the podium at an AA meeting) was met with a collective shrug. My friends already knew or didn't care, and the same went for my mother. Telling my father was more difficult. Though he and I had a loving relationship, I didn't really know him. From the time he and my mother separated, we were almost never within three thousand kilometres of each other, but I knew his voice well enough—I'd been calling him on the phone all my life. When I was a kid, it had to be on Sundays when the rates were cheap, or at least after 6 PM. By the time I was a teenager, the rates had changed, but I still made this call at night, after dark. I wasn't ashamed, but it was awkward to come out to a man I didn't really know.

My father has a wonderful voice, a rich and gentle baritone. That sound had always been the string and he the kite, and I knew that to reel him in all I had to do was pick up the phone. I told him what I had to say, and he said—I quote him exactly because even decades later I can—"I don't care who you love, or how, as long as you have love in your life."

Not everyone accepted me. Indian mystic Bhagwan Shree Rajneesh claimed, among many other things, that homosexuals had fallen from dignity, and he told his followers, known as the orange people, that we were not human. My stepsister, herself an orange person, greeted me on my next visit to her home with a spray bottle filled with rubbing alcohol and purified water to protect her from AIDS.

Ultimately, coming out was a relief, but it only formalized what I was already feeling. Thus declared a homosexual, I was free to go about the messy business of defining myself—and for a while I was defined by combat boots, spiky hair, and an undignified proclivity to pursue girls. Fuck the orange people.

When my mother came out, she was forty. Everything from

her politics to her hairdo to her impressive collection of tools had hinted at it, but she'd always demurred. "Oh, I'd love to be a lesbian," she'd coo and bat her lashes, "but I just can't get it up." This was my mother: direct, saucy—and straight. Until she wasn't. She fell in love with a woman, and I suddenly had two mommies. She was casual about it. It was the 1990s, and queers were here, but it was a problem for me. Oh, not politically, of course, but personally: she was usurping some of my carefully crafted identity. It's one thing, a proud thing, to walk in the Dyke March with your mother when she's straight-but-not-narrow. PFLAG moms rule. It's another when she's gay. When I came out, I dropped a pin outside of her radius. I loved how it felt to follow the pull of my own choices. When she came out, our orbits collided.

We have ways of establishing independence. I moved out. I moved cities. I moved back. My mother and I remained tethered, our lives entwined sometimes comfortably and sometimes not, but with every move, her vagina was among the other pieces of art, boxed and bulging against the seams of a taped-up cardboard bicycle carton. The last time I unpacked it, I was moving in with my girlfriend. Years later she'd break my heart, but on this autumn Friday, we got the keys to our apartment, walked past the towers of boxes, and crawled into bed. It was Tuesday before we finally began unpacking, and a few dozen more Tuesdays before she'd stand in front of my mother's vagina and say, "How attached to that are you?"

It hadn't weathered well. It was only cloth and cotton batting, and over time the fabric had become brittle, cracked, and shot through with fissures. Occasionally, a tear would come loose, and, unable to figure out how to fix the problem, I'd simply push it back between the folds. More than once, an unwitting houseguest had brushed past, causing a threadbare tear to drop to the floor. I finally put it in deep storage, behind the broken-down dryer in the basement.

Three boxes of university papers, a Krazy Karpet, a collection of fridge magnets, and my mother's vagina: I found all of these when we began to pack up the basement in anticipation of our cross-country move. Three years in a dank cellar had left the vulva covered in a thin patina of mould, and when I hoisted it out of the cobwebbed corner, several tears loosened and dropped to the floor. An accusatory bald patch remained. I put it back behind the dryer and decided it was time to call my mother.

She lived alone now, having broken up with the girlfriend when she realized that she'd gained twenty-five pounds. "We started bringing food into the bedroom to liven things up," she'd confided. "But after a while, we'd just eat a tub of ice cream in front of *Law & Order*." As the phone rang, I pictured them lying there in their matching pyjamas, snacks in hand, a living diorama titled "Lesbian Bed Death." Finally, she picked up. It didn't take long to get to the reason for my call.

"Well *I* don't want it!" she said indignantly, as though I'd cold called her during dinner to offer her not her own vagina but a stranger's.

"It's not *my* vagina!" I shot back.

"But you know . . ." Her voice trailed off, and I knew I was not going to like the end of that sentence. "It *is* a piece of feminist history. I think we should donate it."

She meant "you should donate it," of course, and instructed me to call the local women's sex toy store—just the kind of place that might have wall space for vagina art. I balked. She insisted. We negotiated, and a treaty was struck: I would store the piece for one more week, and she would make the phone calls.

Five days later, my mother called, and she was tense. "They won't take it." Her words were clipped. "Here I am, donating a piece of art—a piece of *our history!*—and they couldn't be less interested."

I didn't know what to say. "They'll come around" perhaps, or "They don't know what they're missing!" Instead I said, "Wait, do you mean to say that they declined your offer of one enormous, mouldy vagina, circa 1965?"

My mother was not amused, and in response neither was I. In the weeks leading up to my move, we stubbornly refused to discuss it, as though by doing so we could effectively erase both the conflict and the artifact. Unfortunately for my unwitting movers, the vagina was, in fact, still in existence, lying in wait behind the dryer, ensconced in the damp embrace of ancient lint.

"Holy shit, what *is* that?" The movers had been calling up and down the basement stairs all day. *Yes, I brought you a coffee. No, the dolly's in the truck where you left it. No, the boss said three flights, you douchebag.* But now the voice from below had lost its bluster and had been replaced by something tentative, a little squeaky. I sprinted to the top of the stairs and listened.

"What. This?" Rustle. And then an all-out, open-throated holler followed by the sound of hundreds of flapping wings.

One of the movers had waited until the other was at eye level to waggle the lady parts, and the sudden movement had startled a colony of moths that, like bats, flew from between the folds directly into the other mover's eyes.

After the movers left, I went upstairs to do a final look-through. Our cats were locked in the bedroom, howling, and my girlfriend was hunkered down, her fingers jammed under the door. "I just want them to know we're here," she said. The living room was bare. A jumble of wires lay in the corner where our television had been. In the corner — my office — scuff marks darkened the wall where for five years my feet had shifted. At eye level there was a bloom of holes like buckshot where I'd wrestled with aligning two framed photographs.

The doorway to the basement was open, and for several long moments I stood in the rectangle of darkness. I wanted to move on, no apologies. Later, as the sun washed the back alleys of Vancouver's east side, I made my way to the nearest Smithrite Dumpster. I wasn't quite tall or strong enough to shoulder the piece into the bin, and the steel lid came down on my fingertips. Two weeks later, in our new apartment in a city on the other side of the country, I would still see the yellow bruises on my knuckles.

KEPH SENETT is a freelance writer, editor, and activist whose passions for travel and soccer have led her to play the beautiful game on four conti-nents. Her work has appeared in a range of international publications, including *Bitch* and *Curve* out of the United States, *Pride Life* from the United Kingdom, and Canada's national gay and lesbian news site *Daily Xtra*. Though frequently in transit, she calls an apartment in Toronto's west end home. Find out more at kephsenett.com.

It Could Happen to You

'NATHAN BURGOINE

I NEVER SAW MY future.

That was—and still is—the thing I have the hardest time explaining to my friends who aren't queer. When I was a kid, looking forward past my adolescence and into the future was incredibly difficult to do. I knew I'd never have a wife or children; I never imagined having any sort of family. As for my parents and sister, my goal early on wasn't to build a relationship with them but to escape them. My family wasn't queer, nor remotely queer-friendly, if the endless stream of "poofter" jokes was even a slight clue as to their true feelings. My father was a big man, a former rugby and lacrosse player, and I was none of those things. I drew. I imagined. I had no athletic skill to speak of. I was as complete a riddle to him as he was to me, and it was obvious that neither of us was going to figure the other out. Our only common ground was books, and most of the time it was enough to give us something to talk about when we had no choice but to interact. My mother and I were closer, but even then, she was content to let me be. "He's great. He takes care of himself" is how she'd describe me to other mothers. "I can give him a pencil and some paper and he's set for the day." I knew that most of the people in my life would not react well were they to find out I was gay. That kind of solitude is a weight, and I couldn't see a future that involved anything changing.

So, as a teenager, I stopped looking ahead and lived day to day without planning ahead, ignoring what I couldn't imagine. I was accepted to university at seventeen, and when the offers arrived, I chose the one that was farthest away from my family and moved to Ottawa. In my first year, I gathered my courage and a few friends and came out. It went well with my friends, for the most part, but when it was time to talk to my family, it soured. Once they found out, they cut me off completely. I turned to a few key friends who helped me through what felt like a devastating confirmation of what I'd always feared: I wasn't worth it. I didn't date much — if no one got too close, then no one could leave me was how I saw it. When holidays appeared, I'd throw parties for a group of friends, which we'd jokingly refer to as "Christmas for Losers" or "Thanksgiving for the Uninvited." They became a kind of surrogate family, those early university friends, at a time in my life when I didn't have a family of my own. And even if some of those relationships faded as we grew older, I was happy enough and found that being without a family wasn't so bad after all—if you occasionally had company.

And then I met Dan.

~ ~ ~

We were set up by friends in one of the most convoluted series of connections I've ever seen. My friend Yumi spoke to our friend Jaimie, who was in a band with Pat, who was married to Natalie, who was good friends with Jen, who was Dan's best friend. Somehow, they decided we were compatible and conspired to invite both of us to a group movie night. It was a showing of *28 Days Later* because nothing says romance like zombies, guts, and blood apparently. I didn't say a word to Dan the entire night, too tongue-tied and too cognizant of our being the only two single people in the room. Not to mention the fact that he was so damned cute, had a career in software development while I worked in retail, and was by all accounts a genius. He even had dimples. But there was hope. When he did speak up during the movie, he was funny, criticizing the insanely poor choices the characters in zombie movies always seem to make.

By the time the next movie night arrived, I'd gathered the courage to ask Dan if he'd like to see a movie together—in a theatre, by ourselves. It came out awkward and stilted, and he was quiet a bit too long, so I hastily added, "It just took me twenty minutes to get up the nerve to ask that." This apparently charmed him enough (or he took pity on me), and our first real date happened shortly thereafter. And another after that. We had more in common than I'd thought: our book collections were similar, we liked the same movies, and we'd both grown up in the United Kingdom and suffered through high school with the goal of getting the hell out of there. And then, three dates later, he invited me to have dinner at his sister's house.

The thought of meeting any of his family had me sick to my stomach. I'd always encapsulated my relationship with my own family in brief euphemisms. "We're not close." "They didn't really speak to me for seven years." "We're starting to talk a little these days." I'd dodged the topic of my family with Dan a few times, but when he saw how nervous I was, he once again took pity on me. His sister—and his sister's girlfriend—was hosting the dinner, he told me, and I should relax.

"Your sister's a lesbian?" I whistled. "How did your parents take that?"

"They were fine," he said and gave a little shrug. "It was obviously easier for me, since she paved the way."

I was thrown. That was it? His parents were *fine*? I was still a mess of nerves, but when we arrived, Jan (his sister's girlfriend) turned to Kate (his sister) and said, "Holy crap, he's tall."

"I know," Dan said. "I'm not used to being the short one."

I laughed. "How do you think I feel? I'm not used to being the dumb one."

Jan gave me a knowing look: Dan had graduated university with a literally perfect grade-point average. His sister had graduated before him with a slightly less perfect result—one A among all the other classes in which she earned an A+.

We ate. We talked. We laughed. We had a good time, and I

relaxed. And a couple of weeks later, when Dan invited me to meet his parents for dinner, I only threw up a little.

⚘ ⚘ ⚘

At the same time that I was meeting Dan's family, my father was diagnosed with heart cancer. At this point, I spoke to my family about once a month, though usually only to exchange bad news (my sister's divorce, my father's stroke). The last time I'd seen my family had been months earlier when I'd gone to visit them—alone—for my mother's sixtieth birthday. The more the doctors looked into my father's heart, the worse the news grew. When the doctors started discussing options with success rates of about ten percent, I took the five-hour bus and train trip to Hamilton. When I walked into the hospital room, I handled things the way my family always has—with a kind of dark humour that mostly avoided the real topic at hand.

"There were easier ways of convincing us you had a heart, you know," I said.

"What are you doing here?" my father asked. It wasn't the warmest of welcomes, but I knew it had come mostly from a place of pride—no one wants to be seen in a hospital bed. By the end of the week, when I'd learned enough to know that this would almost certainly end in my father's death, I called my boyfriend—I was still getting used to calling him that—to come spend the weekend with me.

Dan met my father, mother, sister, niece, and nephew a few days before the unsuccessful operation. At my father's funeral, Dan stood beside me and met the rest of my small extended family and a host of other colleagues, friends, and acquaintances. I was asked to speak on my father's behalf, which made me feel like an actor on a stage. I said appropriate things—dodging more honest feelings and memories—about my father's love of knowing facts and winning trivia games, about his favourite book (*Moby-Dick*), and about his whip-crack mind, which made him capable of saying something clever with only a moment to prepare. He was never a man who had to gather his thoughts and he could speak on the fly, sounding confident and collected. Standing there, I had a sick feeling of vertigo that I was describing what I was doing that very second, but I sat down again to warm smiles from people whose names I didn't know. I put on the best show I could but couldn't stop twisting my father's wedding band—my mother had given it to me—and in something of a cruel irony, my skin reacted poorly to it, and I ended up with a giant rash all over my finger by the end of the week.

I learned at the funeral that there were people who didn't even know I'd come out. The phrase "while he was at university" was glibly slipped into conversation as explanation for why I'd been gone for years, and it was a cold shock to realize that I'd been edited from my family's life so easily. I certainly contributed to making that possible—I hadn't once fought to reconnect, and it was really only the birth of my niece and nephew five years earlier that had started any sort of reconciliation, ending nearly seven years of almost complete silence. When the door had been closed to me, I hadn't so much as turned the handle to see if it was unlocked. After the funeral, communication became more frequent and felt a bit easier. It was a little jarring and seemed to skip any discussion of those years I was "at university." But five hours away, and with my boyfriend, I didn't mind as much as I once had.

I moved in with Dan. We bought a car together—I don't drive, but it was something that was ours. We renovated one of the rooms in his house into a library, making his home feel like something we shared. We played videogames, went snowshoeing, and took a trip to Quebec City for my thirtieth birthday. His goofy love of squirrels and chasing frogs at streams and his wonderful dimples (which he hates) all seemed to blur together into months that passed like days.

His parents live down the street from us, and going over for dinner on holidays and birthdays has become something to which I look forward. It was such an alien sensation to be so readily and happily brought into Dan's family. The Christmas after my father's death, we hosted both his parents and his sister and her girlfriend and opened presents together in our living room. There was a brief moment when I was alone in the kitchen with Jan, who said, "I've never seen them so happy."

"Pardon?" I asked.

"Dan. His parents. They're so happy for him, and he's so happy with you."

When I started to sniffle, she threatened to punch me, and we rejoined the group with something close to composure. Life moved on. And although there were moments when I would find myself surprised by how happy I was, most of the time it was just good to be myself, with a man I loved, who happened to have a family who thought I was pretty decent.

Then, in 2005, while Dan was attending a conference in

San Francisco, Canada passed the federal law that gave queer couples the right to marry. I saw a future.

I proposed on Canada Day in the Ottawa International Airport, at the bottom of the escalators, during a high-summer brownout, when he returned from his trip. I jokingly called it mood lighting. In front of not-so-small a crowd (and with a couple of close friends watching, just in case), I assumed the traditional pose, getting down on one knee while he looked at me in confusion.

"While you were gone, the laws changed," I said. "Will you marry me?"

I held out my father's wedding band, which had remained in a box in my drawer since his death.

"You crazy man," he said.

"I really hope that means yes."

"Yes!"

And we were engaged.

We had a small wedding, only forty or so guests, and we'd decided from step one that we wanted something simple but happy. A celebration of our friends and family — a tricky thing for me, of course, though my mother and sister accepted their invitations, and my favourite cousin and his girlfriend were there. We are told that you will remember your wedding for the rest of your life. I will, of course, but there are two things that stand out. The first is typical. We exchanged rings made from my father's wedding band, which we'd had halved and reworked into styles that better suited us and were more understated. It felt right to me to take something from the past and rework it for the future.

The second is a surprising moment that I will always treasure. When my brand new in-laws stepped up to the podium, I marvelled at them. She smiled at him and there was such love in that look that I had to actually pause and take a breath. Then he said the first words of his speech. "Not many parents are blessed with two gay children," he said.

I don't actually know what the next sentence was. Or even the one after. It took everything I had not to burst into tears. It had obviously occurred to me, over the time I'd been with their son, to wonder whether his parents ever felt like they'd missed something or drawn a poor lot. Do any parents really want their child to be gay? I'd never had the guts to ask. I wondered if they lamented the very unlikely possibility of grandchildren. If they censored themselves around co-workers or friends. Did they ever wish—just a little—that one of their kids could give them the whole package? If anyone had the right to be upset, it was them. One gay child, sure. But both? Unfair.

As I'd gotten to know them, I knew that they were wonderful parents. It wasn't that they were tolerant—tolerance is what we give something we dislike but recognize as undeserving of ill will. They weren't accepting either—acceptance is something you reach, something you learn about, roll around in your mind, and then come to terms with. They were—simply—loving. They were parents. They wanted their children to be as happy and as loved as they themselves were. They felt blessed to have these children.

I caught most of the rest of my father-in-law's speech. He said that he and his wife had never seen Dan so happy. He spoke about his daughter, and her finding Jan, and how he was so happy that both his children had found someone. By the end of this speech, glasses high, I'd given up on pretending not to cry, and there was an ache in the back of my throat.

The speeches, and the meal, continued. At our table, I sat with my husband and thought about that old joke told at traditional weddings: don't think of it as losing a daughter, think of it as gaining a son. I gained a whole family that day.

I'm no longer the young man who used to look ahead and see nothing out there for himself. My husband and I are now the godparents—in a very non-traditional sense of the term—to a lovely baby born to two of our closest friends. That they are a family made of a bisexual mother and a transgender mother had a lot to do with our being chosen for the role. "We want her to grow up with an example of other queer people around her," one of her mothers explained.

That, I think, is what family will be for the rest of my life. My family is my husband and me, his parents, his sister and her wife (they have since married), our goddaughter and her mothers, and our good friends who are scattered around the globe but are close in our thoughts. I am loved, and I love them. That's family.

My mother, my sister, and my niece and nephew? Things have gotten better. The euphemisms, however, still hold. We're not close. But Dan and I, if we're somewhere safe, are publicly a family. I hug my husband. I hold his hand. I kiss him in greeting and at partings and whenever I find him adorable, which is often. And I can't help but wonder if there's a kid watching who fears what will happen when his family finds out about him. Maybe that kid can't imagine what kind of future he could possibly have. I hope he sees us. And I hope he knows that we're saying, *This. This could happen to you. And you'll be so lucky.*

'NATHAN BURGOINE lives in Ottawa with his husband, Daniel. His short fiction appears in two dozen publications, including *This Is How You Die, The Touch of the Sea, Boys of Summer, Men of the Mean Streets,* and *Fool for Love.* His non-fiction has appeared in *5x5* literary magazine and *I Like It Like That. Light,* his first novel, is published by Bold Strokes Books. You can find him at redroom.com/member/nathan-burgoine.

I, Didi

DORIANNE EMMERTON

I'VE NEVER THOUGHT THAT I would make a good mother. I'm extremely impatient and have a temper and anxiety issues. I tend to be outgoing in social situations, but they tire me out and I need significant chunks of time to myself on a regular basis.

It's not that I don't like children. At one family-friendly backyard barbecue, I ended up on the bottom of a pile of wriggling kids who had crowned me "the monster" and chased me around until I let them vanquish me. The rest of the adults were engaged in what I assume were mature conversations. But after that I was tired, so I escaped to the front porch, where I could have a cigarette without proving a poor role model to the ankle-biters. Smoking isn't my only non-kid-friendly habit: I also drink and swear and talk about sex a lot.

And I'm busy. I have a day job that I don't hate and it pays the bills. I'm working on my writing and getting short stories published here and there, some of them even resulting in sums of money (albeit smallish sums). I have two ongoing unpaid gigs: one reviewing theatre and one hosting a radio show about sex. That doesn't leave much time for a child. But I'm dating an amazing woman who always wanted to have a baby (for the sake of her privacy, I'll refer to her as The Girlfriend).

The relationship happened by accident. When we first started seeing each other, I was just finishing a long, bad breakup, so I was looking for something casual, light, easy. She was leaving Toronto for school in three months' time. We weren't monogamous. How heavy could it get? It didn't ever get heavy. But it got very real.

Her friends were here, so she came back to visit whenever she had time off school. Her university was only three hours away, so I went to visit sometimes. All of a sudden, two years had passed and we were still together. She moved back to the city—but not in with me. I have a cat whom I dearly love, and she's deathly allergic. And we had both discovered that we enjoyed living on our own. We partied and went to concerts and movies and the theatre. We had political debates and weekends in Montreal. We spent a month travelling in Europe. It was comfortable but never boring. When we argued, we worked it out afterward. We knew how to apologize; we knew how to give each other space. We were in love. And then we had been together for four years. What were we going to do about this pesky difference in opinion about having children?

She started attending co-parenting meetings at a local LGBT

community centre. The idea was for queer people to try to forge a relationship where two (or more) of them could raise children together, without requiring any romantic attachment. But there was a dynamic that The Girlfriend didn't like: there were a lot of gay men who, she felt, were looking for a "rent-a-womb," resulting in a child-share. She didn't want to co-parent with someone she only saw when they dropped the kid off to each other. She didn't want to argue with someone about disciplinary tactics and dietary choices only as problems arose. She wanted to collaborate, to anticipate parenting decisions and make them together. She wanted to have consistent rules and routines and to do things together as a family.

So she and some of the other women from those meetings started a breakout group called Queering Rearing. The idea was to help one another with having and raising children — the "it takes a village" approach. The Girlfriend asked me to come to these meetings. I agreed because it seemed less formal than the co-parenting meetings. I agreed because I had already met most of the people going, considered them friends, and felt comfortable around them. I agreed because I realized that I would necessarily be involved.

A kid takes up a lot of a parent's life. If I was going to date The Girlfriend while she raised a child, I would have to be in that child's life. There were things I liked about the idea: I'd get to play the monster a lot. Maybe I'd get to be the adult they actually liked when they were teenagers. Then they'd ask me about sex and drugs, the things they wouldn't want to ask their mother. She didn't ask me to take on half of the responsibility, half of the expense, or half of the time commitment. It would be *her* child. I would be a person dating someone who had a baby, offering whatever help I could spare from my busy life. Maybe it wouldn't work out and that would be the end of us as a couple. But a relationship can fail for all sorts of reasons. I could imagine being a mother's little helper (the non-pharmaceutical version), so it only seemed fair to give it a shot.

After that, everything went into hyper drive. The Girlfriend got into a graduate program that she really wanted to do. But it required daytime classes and her nine-to-five schedule wasn't flexible. She didn't want to quit her job, especially since it had good maternity leave provisions. Since the coursework was only for one year, and a maternity leave is also for a year, we got busy interviewing sperm donors.

It's illegal to pay for sperm (or eggs, or surrogacy) in Canada, so fertility clinics don't have a wide variety of donors. They do, however, charge a lot of money for the service of inserting the sperm. So The Girlfriend took the DIY approach instead: she picked up some specimen jars and syringes at a medical supply store and started perusing websites where prospective donors posted profiles. She selected some candidates, and I helped to interview them on the phone. The decision was entirely up to her, but I was happy to offer a second opinion.

When we tell people about this, they often wonder about the donors' motivations. Generally speaking, people donate things — their time, their money, their blood — because they want to help others. Often they get into a particular cause because of a specific personal motivation. For example, when a close relative or friend is diagnosed with cancer, a person is more likely to donate to cancer-related causes. Sperm is no different. Most of the guys we met had a person in their life who was queer or had experienced fertility issues, and they thought, Hey, I have something I can give away for free that would really help someone out.

So we found a nice guy who lived in a nearby city and wanted to help The Girlfriend have a baby. He offered to meet us halfway, at a coffee shop off the highway, on the day of that month when The Girlfriend would be most fertile. We were a bit surprised, but he said he had done it before. We met him and gave him the specimen jar. He ducked into the coffee shop washroom and came out a couple of minutes later, slipping us the jar. We sucked the contents into a syringe and inseminated in the back of our rented Honda Civic. Then I drove us back to Toronto.

That was the first try, and it didn't take. The second time, The Girlfriend's optimum fertility day came earlier than expected, so that guy wasn't available, nor was I. She took a train to a different city to meet a different donor and inseminated herself. (There was a dearth of decent Toronto-based donors on the websites. I attribute this to a large city having more opportunities for arrangements to happen socially, but that's just an assumption.) The second time worked, and I'm a little sad I wasn't there for it, despite the fact that artificial insemination takes about two seconds and isn't all that exciting.

Like most people, The Girlfriend didn't want to tell anyone for the first three months. That's when most miscarriages happen so there's an air of superstition — let's not jinx this! — but you also don't want to have to tell everyone when you've gone through something as traumatic as losing your baby. I was in a state of somewhat pleasant anxiety that trimester. I *hate* secrets. I keep other people's, but I don't have any of my own, and this implicated me enough that it was my own as well as hers. And it didn't involve simply not telling people — it involved prevaricating. My book club was planning a trip and I . . . couldn't be away in July. I had a lot of plans in July. It was just a very busy month. Oh, she couldn't make it to tonight's party because she's tired. Because . . . she had a tough week at work. I can't stand lying, so these weren't lies. I was going to be busy in July *helping my partner deliver a baby!* The Girlfriend had a tough week at work *because she had first trimester fatigue and nausea!* I couldn't wait to tell people, and when we finally did, I broke apart.

I became inordinately stressed out by people treating me as the de facto other parent. The fault was partially mine, as I was pretty excited to share the news. But I never said, "We're having a baby." I said, "She's having a baby," and to me, at least, that was a different thing. I didn't understand why our radical queer friends would automatically assume a traditional family model. They knew we didn't live together. They knew we weren't monogamous. A couple of people went so far as to refer to me as "Daddy." That's when I started thinking, What have I done? What have I agreed to? Why didn't I run while I still could? And then I got depressed and started behaving badly. It didn't help that this was late January, early February, already the most dismal time of year.

We found a couples counsellor. She was queer too, but I still worried that she would have some investment in nuclear families. Maybe she'd be horrified by our polyamory. Maybe she'd tell us we were overly ambitious to think our relationship could survive. I'd had a bad experience with a psychiatrist in university, when I was in the throes of figuring out my sexuality, who told me I "thought about humping too much," so I always approach therapy with a little trepidation. Thankfully, our lesbian therapist was wonderful and helped immensely. I'm a big advocate of couples counselling now. Every relationship has its rough patches, and the involvement of an appropriately educated third party is invaluable. The Girlfriend and I are good communicators, but that didn't mean there weren't things we were afraid to say. Our therapist helped clear away the fears so we could see how strongly we were bonded and how much potential there was for this abnormal arrangement to work.

I think we both learned a lot, but the most relevant was something I learned about myself: I can't feel trapped. I need people to understand our deal more than The Girlfriend does because I'm a public person. My life is open to the world and that's both personal and political for me. It's political because I'm convinced the only way to de-stigmatize things like being queer, and being polyamorous, and even just being a woman who enjoys sex, is for people like me (who are privileged enough to be safe doing so) to be open about it. It's personal because I feel constricted and constrained when I have to keep part of my life secret. And I don't react well when I feel that way.

We negotiated plans for the upcoming year of pregnancy, birth, and life with an infant. I would still go on a vacation, without her, that my book club was planning, but I would skip a music festival I usually attend because she'd need my help during that month. I would spend at least three nights a week with her and the baby, but the rest of my time would be at my discretion. As long as I explained to people that we had this arrangement, I felt more comfortable. If they were going to think I was a horrible person, at least it would be based on the actual situation. I was no longer trapped by someone else's expectations. It's not that I'm afraid of people's disapproval. A lot of social conservatives will always disapprove of me because I'm a loud-mouthed, pro-choice, sex-positive, fat-activist, feminist, atheist lefty. But what I'm not is some queer version of a deadbeat dad.

Therapy also helped me realize that I *wasn't* trapped. The Girlfriend could have considered my anti-kid stance a deal-breaker and left at any time. She could have devoted her energy to finding a partner who did want children. She wasn't staying with me so that I would have to help her; she stayed with me because she wanted to be with me. And because she thought this could work.

The Baby was born three days after his due date in July. It was horrible. Prenatal classes had taught us that babies-to-be have their own agendas, so we rolled with it when we had to go to the hospital for The Girlfriend to be induced, even though we had planned a home birth. The oxytocin used to induce birth isn't pretty. It gave The Girlfriend sudden, intense contractions with little or no break in between. This went on and on and on, and there was nothing I could do to make the pain stop for the woman I love. When the midwife told her it could well be another twelve hours, she opted for an epidural. That gave her relief—in fact, she slept. But I had no drugs in me and could not sleep. Instead, I spent the next hours in one of the most dreadfully intense pits of anxiety and despair I have ever experienced. I knew people who had had stillbirths and babies with severe birth defects. Sometimes women still die in childbirth—not often but sometimes. My brain wouldn't stop contemplating the most terrible scenarios. And I was trapped, literally. I couldn't leave the little hospital room because The Girlfriend might wake up at any time. I had to stay there in the dark, with nobody but my own madly spinning mind for company.

Eventually she did wake up, the midwife came back, and The Baby was born. He was fine, but because of some minor complications during the birth, the midwife had us stay at the hospital for observation. It was supposed to be for twenty-four hours, but it stretched into twenty-nine as they waited for blood test results. The nurses kept telling us it would be another hour, and then that hour would pass and we still couldn't leave. I felt trapped again. I was shaking and crying. Luckily, my mother had arrived by that time. I left The Girlfriend with her and fled to a nearby spot to lose myself in a novel. And this is part of why I cannot imagine myself as a parent: I don't have the patience. I don't have the fortitude. I break down so easily. And you can't neglect a child for the relief of a fictional world whenever the going gets tough. This is why The Girlfriend is The Mother.

We all went to my girlfriend's apartment that first night back from the hospital. The Baby would not sleep. He wouldn't stop crying unless someone was walking with him. We traded him back and forth, catching a couple of hours where we could. The next day I was so tired that people on the street must have thought I was a midday drunk because the best walk I could manage was a controlled stagger. But my staggering brought me back to my own apartment. I didn't sleep—I was afraid I would fall so deeply that the alarm wouldn't wake me to be back at the promised time—but it was such a delicious respite to be alone in my own space, in peace and quiet, for a couple of hours.

My mother stayed with The Girlfriend for the week, until her own mother came. My mother helped wash dishes, do laundry, buy groceries, and, of course, care for the brand new child. She kept me sane. She said, "You're so good with The Baby," and it broke my heart. Because what I read into that was: "You can parent this child. And then I get to be a grandmother." The hardest part about not wanting children has always been denying my parents grandchildren. For a while I held on to the hope that my brother would take care of it for me, but that hasn't materialized (yet).

Now The Baby is here, The Girlfriend is in grad school, and I take care of him every other Thursday afternoon while she's in class. I also take care of him for a couple of hours two or three times a week so she can write her assignments. He's three months old and sometimes he's a darling and sometimes he's difficult. When he's determined to be a problem, I put him in the carrier and go for a walk. That always calms him down, and I like to walk too.

The Girlfriend also has class on Wednesday mornings right now, and another friend takes care of him then. Other members of our Queering Rearing group and social networks help with taking care of The Baby, bringing food, and offering other kinds of support. I'm still afraid that the day will come when my nerves will not stand the pressure of his indiscernible needs, his impossible demands. I hear the Twos are terrible. But I think I'll be able to manage it because I only take care of him by myself for defined periods of time. There will always be that light at the end of the tunnel, where he becomes someone else's responsibility and I can go read a book somewhere quiet.

When I'm not with The Girlfriend and The Baby, I still have the life that I didn't want to leave. I see midnight screenings of horror movies, go to concerts, and drink with friends until last call. I review plays and host my radio show. And I'm still doing a lot of writing, even at The Girlfriend's place. I guess a new mommy needs a lot of sleep because she and The Baby go to bed a good two hours earlier than she used to, so I use that time to put words into Word. It's a heavily scheduled existence, but that's fine by me. I'm handy with a Google calendar. Having a full plate doesn't frighten me.

The biggest logistical concern right now is naming conventions. I'm not his mother and I never wanted to be a mother, so I'm not comfortable with any sort of Mommy/Mama/Mom sort of word. And I feel it would be unfair to The Girlfriend, who does the grand majority of the mothering. I'm not masculinely identified, so Daddy/Papa doesn't work (and I probably would be uncomfortable with the full-parent connotation of those words even if I were butchier). We started with Auntie, which seemed fine before he was born but bothered me once he was here. I am far more than an aunt, even if I am neither Mom nor Dad. Right now, we're calling me Didi. My close friends and family call me D, so Didi is just my nickname said twice. It feels comfortable to me, and it still has that caregiver ring. I'm not sure what my parents are yet. They want to be grandparents, but I don't know if that will work for The Girlfriend. We'll have to sort that out. And, of course, as The Baby grows into language and relationship awareness, he will make his own decisions about who is called what and what that means to him.

I'm also more comfortable now because I realize that while some people change their lives to focus on their child, it is possible to integrate a child into *your* life instead. I won't have to give up reviewing theatre to take care of him: I'll just review more kids' theatre so I can bring him. I already read young adult novels, so I'll have lots of books to give him when he gets to that age. Or maybe he won't like books and theatre and instead he'll like cars and sports, and we will have to find people to do that sort of stuff with him. But we can do that. There are people with all kinds of interests in our social networks, and we are not afraid to ask for help.

The fact is that the future is unknowable—always has been, always will be. But it's also manageable. I know that The Girlfriend is very capable of raising The Baby. I think that I am capable of helping because I love that little dude. This isn't a surprise. I always knew that if there was a baby in my life I would love him or her. (Or *them* if that's the pronoun they decide on later in life because I'm totally gender-queer positive.) That was a part of my resistance. Loving a child means that it will be devastating when I fail, as I inevitably will. I will lose my temper, forget something important, miscalculate, say the wrong thing, make the wrong choice. And when this happens, and it affects The Baby, I will break apart.

I hope The Girlfriend and our friends and family will be there to glue me back together. Because I don't want to complicate his life with my volatility. I want his childhood to be perfect. I'm aware that this is impossible, but that doesn't make me want it any less. I've been told that this is the mindset of a parent. Yet I'm not legally a parent, and I'm certainly not a traditional parent. I'm a Didi, and I get to raise a baby half the time and run around to art events and parties or stay home to write the other half. I feel like that's a pretty good deal.

As well as being a writer, DORIANNE EMMERTON is a theatre reviewer and radio show host. Recent publications include short stories in *Friend. Follow. Text* and *Beer and Butter Tarts* Issue #1. Her work can also be found in collections such as *Little Bird Stories Volume II* (eBook only), *Zhush Redux*, and *TOK 6: Writing the New Toronto*. She had a play produced in Gay Play Day 2013 and lives in downtown Toronto.

Finding My Grace

BETTY JANE HEGERAT

IN SEPTEMBER 1999, WE moved our daughter to Edmonton to begin the master of library science program; our dear Elisabeth, the daughter who had been born ten weeks early, a feisty two-and-a-half-pound scrap of a baby girl who'd grown into the brightest, kindest, most loving daughter parents could wish for. Two days later, we moved her brother to Lethbridge to begin a conservation enforcement program. We'd looked forward to the fledging of our three children, and even though we still had our youngest son at home, a twelve-year-old with a gang of friends sufficient to keep the nest soiled, the weekend overwhelmed me. The two empty bedrooms and the sudden threesome at the dinner table felt too much like loss. I had not prepared myself for the bittersweet taste of my children leaving home.

Within a few weeks, I felt the need to visit. In Elisabeth's new digs, furnished with familiar castoffs from home, there was reassurance that she had not moved too far away and I would still be called on for the many things a mother does for a daughter. I was hemming a skirt for her, her dad standing at the window looking out at the view from the twenty-first floor of her residence, when Elisabeth marched to a spot between the two of us and uttered the news that she was seeing someone, and that someone was a girl—a young woman she'd met online. A few years older than Elisabeth, Barb had taught ESL in Japan, flown off to another teaching stint in Korea shortly after the two of them met, but had come home abruptly after a brutal attack in her apartment. Now, their relationship had bloomed to the point where Elisabeth needed us to know. We listened calmly, me still stitching, then put our arms around our trembling girl and told her we loved her. We loved her and nothing would ever change that. When we stepped apart, her skirt dangled from my slacks. I'd stitched it to my knee.

I could not have predicted my reaction to the news that my daughter was gay. I had no difficulty with sexual orientation in all its possibilities. I had gay friends, had known other families whose children had come out, and in my head I was as liberal as I could be. What happened in my heart, though, was a profound grief and fear over how the world would treat my daughter now that she had moved out of the mainstream and into a tributary with a long history of discrimination, exclusion, and abuse. On the way back to Calgary that day, Robert and I could find little to say beyond, *Did you suspect?* In retrospect, I realized that there were signs; the curious absence of boyfriends and some friendships with older women had puzzled me. Robert said that he had assumed that his bright daughter was simply waiting for the right man to come along, and until he did she would not waste time she obviously enjoyed spending with her close-knit group of friends, both male and female. It embarrasses me now to admit that after a long silence, I asked him, *Are you hoping she'll get over it?* He didn't answer, just looked at me and shook his head.

Our two sons reacted to the news of their sister's coming out in exactly the way I wish I had been able to react. They were not surprised or dismayed in any way. In fact, they were more concerned with how their dad and I were handling our feelings. We were dealing with the news mainly with silence. We felt it was not for us to tell the world about our daughter's sexual orientation, even though she assured us it was no secret. Finally, we began to tell family and friends. I was embarrassed by the pathetic sound of my voice when I shared this news with my closest friend, someone who loves my children as I do hers. *Does this mean I'll be expected to march in gay pride parades?* I asked her. But if I couldn't be honest with Dorna, then where could I go? I was embarrassed again that my first thought when Dorna laughed and told me that all would be well was that it was easy for her to feel that way—we weren't talking about *her* daughter.

I am a social worker by profession, well connected when I need counsel about anything personal, but my discomfort was coming from a place that led me instead to my church. I was anguishing over the long period of time in which Elisabeth had carried the knowledge of her sexual identity all alone. I'd asked her if she'd thought to confide in the young female pastor we'd had when she was a teenager and still willing to participate in church activities. She shook her head and didn't offer any words, but her expression said it all—that was one of the last places she would have gone.

I have lifelong roots in the Lutheran Church, held there by my belief that a value system based on the basic tenets of Christianity is a solid one and by the need to hear the familiar music and liturgy that touch something deep inside me. Our pastor at the time was recently retired from his chair as president of the Lutheran seminary in Saskatoon and a wise, compassionate man. He listened thoughtfully and nodded sympathetically when I poured out my fears, and when I paused, he sighed. What the church bid him to tell me—and what his wife would be furious to hear him say, he told me—was that I should accept Elisabeth's sexual orientation, love her unconditionally as always, but counsel her to be celibate. The good news, he said, was that the times were changing, even in the Lutheran Church, where the discussion of sexuality had been a hot item at the most recent national conference. There was serious study going on around the acceptance of sexual orientations other than hetero, the blessing of same-sex unions, and the ordination of gay and lesbian clergy. It would come, he assured me. All would be well. Sometimes young people are simply trying to find themselves. It seemed to me that he was suggesting as well that this might be a phase, that some people do indeed "get over it."

When we met Barb, it became clear that Elisabeth was not dabbling in an alternative lifestyle, having a brief fling, or likely to get over it. These two were kindred spirits who shared a love of writing and a literary taste for fantasy. They were both wickedly smart, curious about the same things, and blessed with irreverent senses of humour. Shortly after Elisabeth's disclosure, they moved into a new apartment together, and a year later, after Elisabeth finished her library degree, they moved to Calgary. Elisabeth had a cover-off position in a corporate library, and Barb landed a job with a training program for ESL teachers. They had a comfortable apartment downtown and a circle of friends that included both Elisabeth's longtime friends and new friends. They were enjoying life, talking about marriage, and I was becoming comfortable with their life together. I admit, though, that when they held hands in public or shared a kiss, I squirmed a little, wanting them to be discreet and looking around for reaction. Apparently I wasn't over it yet.

Meanwhile, my congregation was reacting to an upcoming national church conference at which sexuality resolutions were on the agenda with a ferocity that shredded the hope Pastor Roger had planted when I'd first talked with him. Our delegates to the conference were rabidly opposed, and at a congregational meeting to allow for exchanges of opinion, I spoke out publicly for the first time as the parent of a lesbian daughter. Then I went a step further and wrote a letter for the church newsletter urging compassion and acceptance. The week after the newsletter came out, I had phone calls from two people offering support and an invitation to coffee from someone I had known for many years. The coffee meeting turned into a lecture on why I was wrong. The only road I should be encouraging my daughter to walk was one in service of others. This, the good Christian woman assured me, was the exemplary life many nuns, priests, monks, missionaries, spinster teachers, and nurses had chosen and the world was a better place because of their choices. I could only laugh at how this advice would be greeted by Elisabeth and Barb. But I went away hurt, for them and for myself and for this woman and her beliefs. The resolutions were defeated at the national level, and I began to give serious thought to leaving the church.

Meanwhile, Bill C-38, the Civil Marriage Act, passed, and same-sex marriage became legal in Canada. But with an election looming, and the possibility of a Conservative government replacing the Liberals, Elisabeth and Barb decided that the opportunity might not last and they began to make wedding plans. In August 2006, Elisabeth and Barb were married in the garden at the Deane House, the historical residence of the superintendent of Fort Calgary, now a restaurant. It was a small and simple wedding for family and close friends, the two brides gowned and smiling and leaving no one with any doubt of their love and commitment. They made their own wedding arrangements, but I offered advice on the dresses, ordered bouquets of calla lilies for them to carry, and bossily insisted on being the traditional mother of the bride. Clouds had threatened all morning, but the sun peeked through at the beginning of the ceremony, shone on the words of the justice of the peace and the vows, and then the sky opened just in time to get everyone under cover for the party. Rain on a wedding day—an auspicious beginning. It was a celebration as fine as any wedding can be, and as fine as I'd ever imagined for my children.

Still wounded by the bitterness of the church discussion around blessing same-sex marriage, I attended even less frequently than in my spotty history. My only involvement, aside from the occasional worship service, was a commitment to rebuilding and tending the church gardens. I'd been recruited to the task by Judy, a woman who knew my love of gardens and who had become a fast friend in our partnership over rose bushes and perennial beds. When Judy's son came out, our friendship deepened, and we had long talks from the heart as she went through many of the conflicted feelings I finally felt I had understood and put to rest. We were to become even more united when another national church conference loomed with the sexuality resolutions back on the table.

I spoke out on the issue but with less passion than before. The secular world was doing far better in its acceptance of alternative sexual orientations, and I felt my connection to the church slipping. My children had made their own decisions about church attendance and matters of faith and only came with me on Christmas Eve because they knew how much I would miss having them beside me in the candlelight, singing "Silent Night," before we went home to have our traditional meal and gift-opening. My husband was raised in a Roman Catholic home, probably over-churched as child, and rarely came to church with me. He surprised me, though, by cautioning me not to make any permanent breaks no matter what the decision of my congregation. He felt, he said, that there would be a hole in my life if I did this. Be patient, he told me.

My patience as the national church conference and the vote drew near was more like apathy. I had no power to change the way Lutherans at large felt on this issue, and I tried to respect the opposing position and simply hang on to the belief that it was just a matter of time before things changed. For me, though, it was long past time.

In June 2011, the Evangelical Lutheran Church in Canada voted in favour of the human sexuality resolutions, but the joy I felt was short-lived. The final decision on putting these resolutions into practice was to be left to individual congregations. In my church, I knew there were enough dissenting voices, and more dishearteningly, our new pastor's voice was now added in opposition. He was a young man with a strong connection with the youth in our church, and I was stunned by his position. Because it was such a divisive issue, a two-year moratorium on the decision was declared. Again, I was packing my spiritual bag and preparing to leave. Through all of this churning over my place in the church, I rarely spoke of it to Elisabeth and Barb. They didn't need to be reminded of closed-mindedness and downright odious interpretations of their sexual orientation. I'd been outspoken enough on issues of social justice while my children were growing up for Elisabeth to know that I was not silent on this one.

A few months after the moratorium decision, the issue became more urgent when our pastor left suddenly. How could we call another pastor when we hadn't decided where our congregation stood on the three resolutions? Our church council suggested a committee be struck to present information and education on both sides of the argument, and I was asked to be part of the committee. I knew of at least one person who would be on the committee, someone who had been urging the congregation to join the Solid Ground movement, a group of Lutheran churches who rejected what they referred to as "theological innovations" or Lutheran liberalism and adhered to Biblical literalism. After the first meeting, I knew that there were others who were on the fence, and I had no feeling for which way they would swing. I urged my gardening partner, Judy, to volunteer for the committee, knowing this would be difficult for her because her son's sexual orientation was not known in the church, neither did she feel ready to disclose this personal information. Still, she agreed, and so began eight months of "education."

During that time, we showed films, had speakers on both sides of the debate, and set up a table with articles, books, and DVDs, with the goal of getting people to talk. Through it all I kept trying to get a sense of the general leaning but could not. So, I tried to be patient, which meant stifling my anger. When my comment that we were not talking about people outside our church but about families within who had gay children and were hurting from the lack of inclusion and acceptance, I was met with the comment that there were other families who loved their children equally and showed it by helping them to return to heterosexual lifestyles. Another time, a pastor from the Solid Ground movement who came to speak said there was strong evidence suggesting that many homosexuals chose that path because they had been sexually abused as children and later lowered his voice and reminded us that "what we permit, we promote."

I decided to quit the committee because I felt disconnected and of little use in the discussion. I met with a retired pastor who is part of the congregation, a wise man who had told me that he had totally reversed his position on sexuality issues and now avidly supported acceptance, inclusion, and compassion. After listening to me, he simply shook his head and said, "No, you cannot leave. You must lead by your grace."

My grace? I was counting on God's grace to help me deal with the anger and the hurt I was feeling. Where was that grace that encompasses God's love and mercy, the forgiveness and benevolence that are given freely? I'd attended enough Sunday school and confirmation classes to know that this was one of Martin Luther's quarrels with the Catholic Church. Grace, he said, was bestowed through faith alone. The Catholics had a more complicated view on how one earned God's grace. And I, in the midst of this turmoil within my church, wondered if my faith was sufficient to warrant God's grace. I knew I was meant to follow God's example and take that love, mercy, compassion, and forgiveness into the world. I decided that if this man for whom I had so much respect had confidence in my ability to lead, I would see my involvement through to the vote in spite of the doubts about what I believed or could continue to believe.

On October 28, 2012, after the Sunday worship, we held a special congregational meeting to vote on the three resolutions. The church was full, and when I looked around at the number of grey heads, the people for whom this had been their spiritual home for several decades, I resigned myself to leaving them in peace. We voted by secret ballot, then adjourned for coffee while the votes were counted. I kept myself to the people I knew supported the resolutions and closed my ears to the other conversations around me. It was too late to worry. When we went back into the sanctuary, Judy and I sat in a front pew. All three resolutions passed, all with more than eighty percent support. We had just become the only affirming Lutheran Church in Calgary apart from the U of C campus ministry. And if this could happen in my church, this act of inclusion, of true grace, it would happen in other Lutheran churches.

It has taken fourteen years for me to feel that I am finally in step, ready for the parade. On Christmas Eve, when my family attends church, we will all know that we are in an accepting place. If the two beautiful wives sitting beside me embrace each other during the service, I will smile and I will not need to look around me for reaction. I have found grace within and without.

BETTY JANE HEGERAT is a social worker by profession but for the past twenty years has actively pursued a career in writing. She completed her MFA in creative writing through UBC in 2008. Her fiction has been published in literary magazines and anthologies. Her books include *Running Toward Home* (NeWest Press 2006), *A Crack in the Wall* (Oolichan Books, 2008), *Delivery* (Oolichan Books, 2010), and *The Boy* (Oolichan Books, 2011). She lives in Calgary.

Like Christmas
and Birthdays

PAUL AGUIRRE-LIVINGSTON

DECEMBER 25, 2012. IT'S Christmas Day, and I'm sitting alone in a three hundred dollar hotel room I can't really afford. The sheets are Egyptian cotton, but the wine is as cheap as it can be. *Grand Hotel,* the 1930s film about a group of strangers living in a Berlin hotel starring Greta Garbo and John Barrymore, plays on mute, with a sunken, lifeless sepia tone that seems to match the mood my life has taken on. I like to watch the expressions and imagine my own storyline, one with colours and texture.

I've been asked to contribute to this anthology on modern queer families after a year in which I doubted I'd ever been part of one, feeling cheated, battered even, by the very concept itself. At last night's family dinner, the first one I'd attended in two years, I barely managed a greeting before retreating to the basement. By now, it's also been one month since I've seen or had any meaningful interaction beyond a text message with Noah, my best friend of twelve years. Noah and I met at the cusp of my teenage sexual awakening, as I unsophisticatedly navigated the nature of loving and being loved, for better or for worse, by people you unabashedly believed were required to be there for you, if only because you'd be there for them too.

Most people blindly accept the truth that we're given only one set of parents, and we rarely stop to think about what that means until there's a break in the system. I was lucky enough to have two sets of parents. But, like most of the best things in this world, "the family" is an idea widely held as a right instead of a privilege. I often think of family as a privilege that, especially as a gay man, I'll always have to fight for and still might never get.

In my short years, I have never felt more alone than I do now, sitting in this hotel room, experiencing a solitude I never believed could exist because I had parents who loved me and friends I would die for.

♃ ♃ ♃

December 25, 1994. By my eighth Christmas, I had lost both of my biological parents. A few months prior, a week to the day after my birthday, my father had succumbed to a short, ruthless battle with cancer; my mother, on the other hand, was sixteen when she gave birth and barely stuck around for my first birthday. These Christmases remain like cigarette burns on my brain—not as holes in clothing but as scars on skin.

This one I remember as being particularly difficult because of the sombre mood lingering about. It's the type of mood I'm reminded of when there's garbage in desperate need of being taken out, the kind of garbage consisting of fresh food scraps that produce a faint stench that wafts upon entry, but that your senses calibrate to fairly quickly and effortlessly. I always found loving and relating to people, especially my family members, to be like that.

My childhood was a lot of this: competing bouts of hope and sadness that bred resilience. The only things that saved me were my paternal grandparents, along with my father's three younger siblings. They were my surrogate family. Immediately after my mother unceremoniously bowed out of my life, my father and I went to live with them. I was raised in their home without hesitation, doubt, or regret. My biological parents were children themselves, and it was understood as a familial duty that all hands would be required on deck in my rearing.

I remember it as an erratic household. We lived on the outskirts of Jane and Finch, one of Toronto's most nefarious neighbourhoods of the decade, in four bedrooms with seven people spanning three generations. It was always full of life and sounds—a constant cacophony of Western influences blending with, and clashing against, traditional Chilean heritage and ideals. I grew up in the middle of it all. Spanish was the primary language of the house, so it became my mother tongue. Both of my grandparents worked long hours in trades—he as a general contractor, she at an automotive assembly plant—so I also learned the value of a dollar. We weren't exactly middle class or a conventional household, but we didn't live off the system, and my grandparents took pride in that above all else. Homes like ours were common in our diverse, immigrant-rich pocket of the city.

Shortly after we formed this mutant breed of extended family, my twenty-four-year-old father relocated to Vancouver in search of work, where construction was booming. I didn't go with him; he couldn't raise a toddler on his own. Yet I never felt his absence as any sort of void; instead, my father's siblings became my own brother and sister instead of uncle and aunt. I came to call my grandparents Mami and Tati, or Mom and Dad. I was not only one of them, I was *theirs*. For now, forever.

♌ ♌ ♌

December 24, 1997. Three years after my biological father's death, I remembered him mostly as a man undergoing chemotherapy treatments. He was twenty-seven when he passed away, and no one had quite recovered from the loss. We didn't mope about wearing black like good Catholics, but I remember a palatable change when, upon turning eleven, I asked for a birthday cake with buttercream icing, like all the Canadian kids in my class brought to school, and all Mami could cook up were tears and a heavy heart about how distraught I was expected to be feeling. But I don't remember feeling much of anything. I only remember how hard I willed life (and birthdays) to go on as usual.

It was around that Christmas that Christine, my biological mother, reappeared as a consistent figure in my life, or as consistent a figure as a twenty-six-year-old former teenage deadbeat could be. There were hard feelings, but not from me.

When I was three, Christine had instigated a custody battle out of the blue; who knows why, but I like to imagine that the guilt of failed motherhood was crushing her from within. One evening, Christine showed up at our door with police officers, a lawyer, and a court statement alleging that my father had removed me from her custody without approval and denied her visitation, a statement that would be held as truth until proven otherwise in family court. I remember uncontrollable, blaring wails from all corners of our modest living room. I remember a female officer pleading with Mami to hand me over; I remember clinging to her harder than a kid who didn't want to go to school. At times, if I think deeply enough, I can even remember what I think is my own face. It paralyzes and threatens to unravel the tiny pieces that seem to hold me together as an adult.

Back then, Christine was a stranger I didn't want to go with, but I had to. For the next six months, we lived in a trailer park in a tiny town far from Toronto until my father, in a rare decision, won sole custody on the strength of his family's testimony and the judge's thoughts that they would provide a more stable environment for my upbringing. (The judge has most certainly passed on, but I am forever in his debt.)

It was for this reason that my grandparents had no intention of ever forgiving Christine, and it was understood that I wouldn't either. Yet, to quell any angst I might face as a teenager, my grandparents encouraged us to have regular communication and visits. They were simple and uncomplicated when they took place, as she frequently postponed our plans in favour of some boyfriend or whatever.

When my father passed away, it was decided for me that

I would continue to tell Christine he was still working in Vancouver until the pre-arranged legal guardianship papers were finalized. She would ask how he was doing, and I would say he was fine. When she came to pick me up, she would ask if she could see him, and I would say he wouldn't be home until the following month. (She never, ever came the following month.) For an eleven-year-old, the lie came easily. But on this Christmas Eve, my grandparents told me it was time to tell the truth because I would finally be safe from her potential meddling.

When Christine took me home that night after visiting with her mother—a new tradition that I came to like because I could eat turkey and gravy, items seen as blasphemous to any self-respecting South American, especially on holidays—my parents awkwardly invited her in for tea. In the glare of tinsel and Christmas lights, I sat across from her and explained what had happened over the past three years. To this day, after having broken the hearts of men who barely even deserved it, I have never caused anyone more pain. *Why?* she kept asking us. Why didn't we tell her the truth? Why did they think she would cause problems? Why wasn't she able to say goodbye to her first love, the father of her only child? There were no answers.

September 4, 2002. The years following my disclosure to Christine coincided with my ascent into adulthood. I spent the majority of this time trying to navigate and make sense of having two sets of parents: one through biology and one through circumstance. One very real, and one that was never fully available to me. It was also the time I began to discover my sexuality, with a dizzying schedule of covert rendezvous and experimentations fuelled by the blossoming Internet Age that connected men seeking men in ways like never before. But the early days of Internet dating were riddled with paranoia, and this spread, unfounded, to my offline life.

The unapologetic, fiercely unconditional love that protected me as a child did even more for me as a gay youth. I was raised to strive for more, to surmount tragedy and doubt, and this meant that I never really had to discuss being gay with anyone because we had been through bigger, more important wars. When I told my sister, just before my fifteenth birthday, she laughed in my face at how serious I was being. And "so what?" became our mantra. My parents weren't deaf or blind either, and any questions about my "unique tastes" were few and far between. The constant fight to let me grow up like my peers—to balance and develop my own worldviews counter to my grandparents' 1960s-era beliefs—was quickly won in my favour. After all, I always got what I wanted for fear that any gaping voids would trigger a black hole of post-adolescent fuck-ups.

As I began to talk less to my parents about everyday, some-times gay, things, Christine understood more. She was privy to my new tastes in clothing, in hairstyles, in pop music, in extracurriculars with men, in piercings, in the Spice Girls. She did things with me that my aging parents didn't want to do, like take me to my first concert (a Britney Spears show in a neighbouring city). Even though my parents didn't approve of so-called hard rock and words like *fuck*, Christine bought me Alanis Morissette's *Jagged Little Pill*, which basically shaped my entire worldview before Joan Didion, Malcolm Gladwell, and Simone de Beauvoir. In what my parents thought was her most aggravating move, she took me to see Demi Moore in *Striptease* because I asked her to.

I could count on one hand the number of people who knew the intimate details of my situation—not only that I was gay, but also that I had a vaguely sad, torrid past that came with a young, certainly crazy biological mother. I didn't drink or smoke; I was an honours student and a nice boy. My only rebellion was having a secret relationship with my biological mother that I couldn't possibly tell my parents I enjoyed.

December 24, 2007. By the time I turned twenty-one, I had moved in and out of my parents' home a couple of times before finally making a go of it on my own as I neared the end of my university studies. It had also been one year since I'd had any contact with Christine, who had left me a voicemail in the early hours of my twentieth birthday and changed her number by the time I tried to call her back. I was puzzled, but it didn't really faze me. She had come and gone like a series of Indian summers. I had found new people to share my interests, and I had previously functioned just fine without her anyway. Plus, I had this novel independence to relish: a new loft downtown, a one-year anniversary with my boyfriend, graduation, and my first internship.

I could easily have found Christine if I'd wanted to. I could have emailed her, or visited her apartment, or called her mother. But I didn't. I decided to leave her behind. Similarly, I became determined to leave any traces of my complicated childhood behind as well. It was time to live by my own rules. I was as cunning, ambitious, reckless, and naive as they came. And so, as much I didn't need to, or even want to, I found myself alienating my parents, in search of a sense of self, a sense of independence.

September 4, 2008. If friendships and partying can be viewed as life support, then I'd been on it for a year, along with my two best friends. Pam and I became roommates when she left a decade-long relationship with her high school sweetheart after a year of marriage when she discovered her wife had cheated. I introduced her to my first gay friend, and my only best friend, Noah, who himself was the product of a broken home. His mother had left his family to move across the country, and his father had slipped into a lengthy depression, leaving him and his older sister to raise themselves. For these reasons, we understood each other beyond words and feelings, the way we understand stars in the sky as forming constellations: they just do.

It was also around this time that one of my most significant romantic relationships had not just cracked but shattered all over my life. I suddenly found myself with an unmanageable panic caused by the demands of what is actually required of a person to be a "significant other." I began to grasp, in ways I wasn't comfortable with, the role one can play in the lives of those with their own perfect snapshots of how you belong in their future—a future, it turns out, that you have very little say in designing. My boyfriend had become weary of the strain he felt from my two best friendships. After ignoring them in favour of him, I decided it was time for a change. I remember the catalyst being a social anthropology lecture exploring the notion of fictive kin—the families and relationships we create for ourselves beyond bloodlines and marriages. I threw myself into this concept wholeheartedly and cast aside anyone else who merely wanted Facebook-depth connections.

Pam, Noah, and I affectionately dubbed ourselves The Trinity, and much of my early twenties was spent doing anything and everything with them, including a lot of things we'd have been better off not doing. It became a never-ending series of episodes of binge drinking, fist fighting, crying, trips to New York, trips into back alleys, professional trials, and all the things best friends do as seen on television. It was during this stretch that I began not talking to my parents for weeks at a time. Pam and Noah became the family I had always wanted, probably because I built them from the ground up and didn't have to navigate them like a foreign language. I felt incredibly, unequivocally fulfilled.

September 4, 2011. The milestone that was supposed to be quarter-life coincided with The Trinity's golden years coming to a close. The deterioration of our familial unit began when Noah and I were laid off within months of each other, as I understand it does with most traditional marriages. What should have been a time of reinvention and support became a stage for our bitterness about life, about the world, about ourselves, about each other. It took its toll. With the temporary help of medication,

I recovered from a mild hit of depression and became serious about a career as a freelance writer, throwing myself back into work. Noah entered his first serious relationship and opted to remain jobless for a year while helping out at his boyfriend's business. Pam got a promotion to management and found herself with little time for much else.

Whatever free second we did find was used to keep The Trinity alive. In many ways, it was too late—the dynamics had shifted and allegiances re-evaluated. Noah began doing everything and anything with someone else, and it caused insurmountable tensions within our relationship. I felt cast aside and ignored, and Noah made no effort to quell my fear that he had "different priorities" and "a new number one" in his life. They were the same arrogant, newly-in-love statements I had made once upon a time. Averting a similar situation was what had brought us together in the first place. Throughout my romantic problems, I discovered that friendships usually survive the relationships for which they are sacrificed. I never wanted to make those sacrifices again, but I've yet to be happier with any other decision I've made.

Still, it was too late. Noah and Pam, who were roommates at the time, were no longer on speaking terms; the resentment was so thick it was suffocating. As I tried to play mediator, I found myself in familiar territory, with a terrifying loneliness creeping back in. The unit I had come to depend on as my new family was disintegrating before my eyes. The bonds and relationships I had come to count on were being trampled and ignored. There was no dwelling allowed, only growing up and moving on, even though I wasn't ready to let go.

I thought The Trinity was my second chance at a family where there were no secrets and doubts, no letdowns and fear—only mutual understanding. I wanted a family I could grow old with since I had resigned myself to the fact that I would probably never have children or choose to be married. Noah and Pam were supposed to be the family I could count on once the parents I loved so much were gone. I was lost.

December 25, 2012. German poet Friedrich Schiller wrote: "It is not flesh and blood, but the heart which makes us fathers and sons." It's these unique relationships that not only give us life but define us; they show us compassion and offer salvation to even the most convincing skeptic. Family, I've learned, is usually a struggle for redemption and reconciliation, bridging the gaps between what-ifs and why-nots to make peace with the past and wake up to the present. No obstacle, no matter how grievous or paralyzing, has to define or enslave the person you want to become. Family is, above all, a means to an end in your journey of self-discovery, a testament to the real gift of second chances.

At twenty-six, I have begun a journey to consider reconnecting with my biological mother before our estrangement spans a decade. She has her own family now, and I have a half-sister who wouldn't even remember me if we met again. Perhaps Christine has more children; I don't know. In many ways, I find comfort in her being in the middle of her own second chance at raising a family, to be there for her child in ways she was never there for me. I want to look her in the face as an adult after all these years, to engage her in thoughtful conversation about the past. I want answers about it all. I want to know what my father was like, how she remembers him. I want to find out if, after everything, she's finally as happy as I will let her be.

In a time when we question "family values," when people feel an institution like marriage is somehow in danger because it's adapting to meet the needs of an evolving society, I can tell you what the modern family looks like: fragmented and fragile but loyal and enduring. It's confusing, and it isn't perfect—but it's wonderful. Whether it's the family you don't choose, or the family who gives you shelter, or the fictive kin we surround ourselves with as adults, the virtue will remain the same. As my parents circle seventy, I fear I still have a long way to go as we reignite the flame in our adult relationship. I feel the same about the few close friendships I have left. But it's never too late. But these kin, fictive or otherwise, are worth fighting for.

PAUL AGUIRRE-LIVINGSTON is a writer and essayist currently residing in Berlin, Germany. For two years, until 2013, he was a weekly columnist with *The Grid* magazine, chronicling Toronto's nocturnal pulse and exploring how different communities often unite to create vibrant cross-cultural nightscapes. His work, on everything from arts to queer evolutions, has appeared in publications like the *Toronto Star*, *The Genteel*, *In Toronto*, *Toronto Standard*, *Toronto Life*, *Filler Magazine*, and more. He has fourteen tattoos, mostly quotations from favourite novels.

More Than a Donor

NANCY NEWCOMB

"I DON'T HAVE A dad, do I, Mom?" my five-year-old daughter, Natalie, asks as we walk away from the school playground.

"Well," I say, hesitating in my own uncertainty, "not like Neko or Julia." Neko and Julia have dads who stand in the schoolyard every morning. They hold backpacks and give kisses.

"Other Mom and I are your parents," I continue. "But remember I said it takes a man and a woman to make a baby? We did have a man help us make you."

"Who was that again?"

"Jay, like your middle name."

"Oh right," she says. I'm ready to explain more, but she's moved on. She's found a big leaf with a hole in it; she holds it to her face like a Mardi Gras mask.

I am confident in telling her she has two moms. After all, she does. I have no doubt that my wife and I are both mothering this child. Two moms go to parent-teacher interviews, cuddle before bed, and take her on vacations. On weekends, she crawls into bed and snuggles up between Mom and Other Mom.

But does she have a dad? There is Jay, of course: he is more than a donor but not quite a dad. I'd meet Jay in hotel rooms in Toronto: he'd come, we'd chat; I'd leave, he'd cum. In the lobby, we'd hug before saying goodbye. He'd go back to his day, and I'd go back to the room to self-inseminate. He put as much effort into making this child as I did. Does that make him a dad? I'm not sure what to tell my daughter because I'm not sure myself.

A few weeks after Natalie asks me that question, the man who made her possible arrives for a visit. He is also the donor of Natalie's older sister, Emily, who is now nineteen and takes great pride in the man she considers her father. Emily picks Jay up at the airport on a Saturday night. The two of them have much to talk about. They are a lot alike, intellectual chatterboxes, an interesting study in nature versus nurture. When they arrive at our house, we exchange hugs while Natalie hangs back. She hasn't seen him since a short visit when she was three, a visit she barely remembers.

We go out to a family restaurant: me, my wife, our girls, and the donor dad who connects us all. Thanks to Jay, each of us at the table is related to one another. We are a very queer family indeed. Whenever we see Jay, we take the opportunity to study his face, his features. What did our children inherit from him? He looks at their faces and mannerisms with the same interest. I also know that he is proud of these girls.

Later that night at home, after Natalie has had a chance to warm up to Jay, they build a Lego city. They talk and laugh; there's no denying there's something special about it. Natalie invites him in for a bedtime cuddle, something normally reserved for Other Mom and me. We hear chatter and laughter from the bedroom, and I feel grateful. This was the ideal scenario for our family, and seven years earlier I had almost given up hope.

Our family came together in an unconventional way. My wife had been a sperm runner between Jay and another woman, the go-between in an attempt to keep things anonymous. Over the course of several months, they got to know each other. Sharon liked him and asked if he would consider being the donor for her and her then partner. She got pregnant on the first try. Seven years later, I met Sharon at the Halifax Pride March, a six-year-old girl on her shoulders. Five years into our relationship, I too was ready to have a child, so Sharon called Jay. Though contact was infrequent, they'd stayed in touch. There were visits, phone calls, gifts, and cards. He said he was willing to do it again, but we all knew it would be challenging. He lived in another province and was busy writing a book and caring for his ailing mum. We had our first opportunity to try on our summer vacation in 2004 when we were in Toronto to see Madonna. I had been tracking my cycle for months, taking my temperature each morning to track my ovulation. The timing wasn't perfect but not so far off that it was impossible. It was the first time I had sperm in my body, and I felt certain I was pregnant. In reality, it would take another year and a half and seven more tries.

Plan B was always in the back of my mind. When a year passed without success, we booked an appointment at a fertility clinic. When I told the doctor I'd been trying for a year already, she asked if I had come into contact with any sperm. I wanted to laugh and tell her, "We're lesbians, not morons." I had all the tests and browsed through the online catalogue of donors. Although looking at profiles was fun, I had my heart set on making it work with Jay. But obstacle after obstacle meant missed opportunities month after month, and missed opportunities meant heartache.

Jay came to Halifax in September 2005. It was a great visit but not one that resulted in a pregnancy. Realistically, we couldn't expect him to fly to Halifax for one week every month. On the other hand, we couldn't afford to have both Sharon and I fly to Toronto every month either. I agonized over Plan B. I knew I'd love my baby no matter how he or she came to be, but every time I came close to making a decision to call it off with Jay and use an anonymous donor, I'd find myself emotional, crying, and not knowing why I felt so strongly about it. But every failed attempt and missed opportunity left me feeling frustrated and helpless. The clinic taunted me with its closeness and predictability, and with every disappointment I would decide it was time to try closer to home.

I wasn't against unknown donor insemination. My friends had just had a beautiful baby girl that way. But I liked the sense of extended family there was with Jay. On a trip to Ontario to visit Jay and his mum, we looked through photo albums and listened to family stories. We got to see the pride in their eyes when Emily played her clarinet for them. I wanted that connection for my child too.

In February 2006, I flew to Toronto alone. With the flight, hotel, taxis, and food, it ended up costing about the same as a trip to the clinic and was a hell of a lot more work. On that visit, I barely saw Jay. We had a few short conversations in the hotel room and then smiles and hugs in the lobby. Two weeks later, I was shocked and enormously relieved to see two pink lines on a plastic stick. It had worked. I called Jay and left a message. We didn't talk to him again until the day Natalie was born.

And now he's here with us for a visit, spending time with the girls he helped create. We go to Fort Anne in Annapolis Royal. Jay, a historian, tells us all about cannons, forts, and wars. Natalie runs up and down the rounded mounds of grass and climbs on the cannons. She asks him questions, then runs off before he finishes answering.

"Do you know which was the smallest cannon, Mom?" Natalie asks me at bedtime cuddle. "The ones at the wooden fort," she tells me. She's referring to the cannons at the Habitation at Port-Royal. I guess she was paying attention.

By the end of Jay's visit, he and Natalie have built a Lego city that covers the entire dining room table. On Wednesday, I drive Jay into Halifax to spend time with Emily. She shows him her university campus; they walk the city and stay up late talking. We meet him again on Friday night. It is the day of Natalie's sixth birthday, the first one Jay has been present for. At the restaurant, Jay makes a toast to Natalie. He gives her two change purses with matching bracelets. His mum, who had passed away in the summer, had picked them up for her. Sharon and Jay discuss Emily's education. Natalie draws Jay a picture. After dinner, we drop him off at his friend's house and get out of the car to say goodbye. "Come give Jay a hug," I say. Natalie runs the other way. Then, just as I'm leaning in to hug him goodbye, Natalie flies between us and wraps her arms around his waist. "Group hug," she says. The hug is tight and sincere.

For her birthday, Natalie receives a gift certificate for our local bookstore. The children's section is full of books with fairies, princesses, and talking pigeons who should not be riding buses. She chooses a children's book on the history of Canada at war. She cannot be talked out of getting this book and listens intently while I read about trenches and tanks. I can't help but read something into her interest in history.

"Mommy, why do I have blond in my hair and you don't?" Natalie asks when we lay down to cuddle. She sounds very concerned.

"You got that from Jay. Jay had blond hair when he was a kid."

"That's when he had hair," she says. She seems happy with my answer, and I smile at her response.

"Mashayla said you can't have two moms unless one of them is a step," Natalie tells me later in the week.

"Well, that's not true," I say. "Other Mom and I are both your moms."

"That's what I told her," Natalie says, a confident six-year-old who's not yet questioned her world. Natalie isn't upset by her friend's comment. "I like having two moms," she says. "It's what makes me different."

I hope she always feels that way, but it's not easy to be different. I know that. And though I know she is growing up in a more open-minded world than I did, my baggage is packed with a fear that she will be hurt by those who don't understand.

She is getting to an age where others are asking questions. I know I have to equip her with the best answers, but I'm not always sure what they are. Our non-traditional family doesn't have a traditional lexicon to fall back on. We are defining ourselves and searching for the right words to help people understand. At the end of the day, the words don't really matter. She'll always know where she came from and how much she was wanted. She will decide for herself how to define her relationship with Jay just as she defined her relationship with her other mom. She is the product of a lot of effort and a lot of love, and no matter the labels of the individuals, as a unit, we are a family.

NANCY NEWCOMB lives in Wolfville, Nova Scotia, with her wife, Sharon, daughter, Natalie, beagle, Scooter, and dachshund, Piper. The family enjoys frequent visits from stepdaughter Emily and pet parrot Sigmund. Nancy has degrees in English from the University of New Brunswick and journalism from the University of King's College. She has been published in several local newspapers. Nancy is currently devoting herself to the two things she loves most: writing and being a mom.

Uprooting a Family: Our Journey to Find a Home

NOREEN FAGAN AND SEBASTIAN CHARGE

Noreen's Story

Growing up as a white girl in central Africa, I spent my days playing with cars, climbing trees, and re-enacting cowboy scenes with the neighbourhood boys. I never wore a dress, except on Sundays when we went to mass. But being a tomboy in Zambia is not unusual. Most of the women I know who grew up there know how to drive across a crocodile-infested river, winch a car out of a muddy pothole, and plug a radiator hole with an egg.

Still, I should have seen the signs. I had fewer crushes on boys than girls, and I never lost my love for all things butch.

But just as I was starting to figure myself out, my mother died in a car crash and my world fell apart. So, at twenty-one, I gave up trying to discover who I was. Instead, I met a man, fell in love, got married, and had two sons, Sebastian and Addison. Sometime between having my two sons, I realized that the crushes I had on women in books and movies had transferred to people in real life—crushes that wound their way into erotic dreams.

The funny thing was, I still couldn't put two and two together to sum up my sexuality. My sister, Frances, tells the story of my father realizing that his youngest daughter was a lesbian and telling her someone needed to tell me. That someone should be her, he said. So, she duly made the phone call that, in Frances's words, was a short exchange ending in denial and a dial tone as I hung up on her.

My transition to homosexuality was long. During my coming-out period, I moved from Kitwe, a small mining town in the northern part of the country, to the sprawling capital city Lusaka for work. I lived there during the week while the boys stayed at home with their father and our housekeeper. Our weekend reunions were great for mother-child bonding but less so for spousal matrimony. Eventually, the deepening chasm widened to a point of no return. I came home one weekend to find that my clothes had been packed up and moved out. I was banned from seeing the boys, my "perverse ways" touted as being detrimental to my sons' mental health.

After my father intervened, I was eventually "allowed" to see my children, and once again, my precarious life of living in two places continued, until my husband and I swapped roles.

The boys would spend their time with me during the week and go to Kitwe, to stay with their father, on the weekends.

Our marital crisis came to a head when my father died. I flew back to Kitwe with his ashes for the funeral and spent the night at our matrimonial home for the first time in years. It was a night marked by sexual threats, fights, and the unmistakable reality—for both of us, this time—that my sexuality was the cause of our breakup. After the funeral, we cut ties and began an uneasy truce. My sons continued to live with me, and under a tacit understanding that my lifestyle was to be kept quiet, my husband and I continued to live our own lives. The truce ended when, eight months after my father's funeral, I asked for a divorce.

My husband promptly resigned from his job, refused to pay child support, and fought for custody of the boys. Our first foray into court was an unpleasant reminder that being a lesbian in Zambia is potentially dangerous. The first argument put forward by my husband's lawyer was that my sexual orientation was unnatural and I was unfit to have custody of the children. It is an argument that might not resonate widely in a North American court, but in Zambia, homosexuality was—and still is—illegal and the threat of imprisonment was real. Same-sex sexual activity is described under Section 155 of the Penal Code Act as an "unnatural offence," and homosexual sex is classified as "carnal knowledge of any person against the order of nature." Any person found guilty of committing a homosexual act may be imprisoned for fourteen years. But in order for someone to be successfully prosecuted, there have to be photos of him or her having sex with a person of the same sex. There were no such photos of me — something to be said for iron gates, burglar bars, and high security (armed burglaries were not uncommon and having security guards on your property was the norm) — so the case was thrown out by the judge, and for better or worse, I remained married, with our divorce on hold. Our boys continued to live with me, and although we were forced to move several times due to financial hardships, we were blessed with a group of friends who supported us.

Life changed when I met the woman who was to become my life partner. Tamara came into our lives when the boys were nine and six. We had known each other for two years, were casual friends who graduated to friends with benefits, and then, in true lesbian fashion, moved in with each other six months after first going out. It was a good life: the boys went to a private school, we lived in a house with a swimming pool, and we were a happy family — albeit a family who remained in the closet. But looming over us was the fact that Tamara was an American on a work permit that was about to expire.

In 1998, Tamara was working for CARE Canada and applied for a job with the organization in Zimbabwe. The country, at the time, was thriving — President Robert Mugabe had not yet cracked down on whites, gays, political opponents, or anyone else who got in his way. Tamara got the job, and plans to move to Harare were put into place, until the country director found out she was in a same-sex relationship and rescinded her job offer. Although CARE has a non-discriminatory clause in its policies, it also has a clause that stipulates the organization must abide by the laws of the countries it operates in, and in Zimbabwe, homosexuality was illegal.

Tamara was devastated and angry. Fortunately, her imme-diate boss supported her and offered her a one-year contract working with refugees, which extended her work permit—and our lives together—for another year. But after that, she found herself on the job hunt once again. She applied for a position with Ipas, an international reproductive rights organization based in North Carolina. Scarred by her previous experience, she was circumspect about our family arrangement in the interviews. Fortunately, Tamara got the job and left Zambia in August 2000. The boys and I made our way after her a month later, not knowing if we would be able to remain in the United States, given that we were foreigners and unlikely to be legally recognized as a same-sex family.

The transition from Africa to the United States was turbu-lent. Getting off the plane and walking into the hot, humid air of North Carolina was like walking onto a film set—a set that we could recognize as being American, but one where there were no cues on how to act, adjust, or understand the culture. Our new home was to be in Carrboro, a small town adjacent to Chapel Hill. The politics of Chapel Hill-Carrboro and its people were liberal; they were accepting of and unfazed by our family. The area is an anomaly in the otherwise Republican state, a liberal haven that has the distinction of being the town with the highest concentration of PhDs in the country and about which the late Republican Senator Jesse Helms said, when asked his opinion on a new state zoo, "Why do we need a zoo when we could put up a fence around Chapel Hill?" But the liberal nonchalance that existed in Carrboro did not extend beyond the confines of the town's boundaries, and trying to enrol the boys in school showed us just how conservative North Carolina really was.

Tamara went to enrol the boys at Lincoln Center, the administrative centre of the Chapel Hill-Carrboro school board, and encountered the first hitch — the not-so-subtle nuances of immigration policies. I came to the United States on a temporary visa (a tourist visa that was changed to a student visa after I was accepted into college six months after we arrived), and so I was not regarded as a permanent resident of North Carolina and neither were the boys. Children could only be enrolled in a public school if the parent or legal guardian was a resident of the state. As their mother, I had no standing in the state, and since Tamara was not their legal guardian, the only way they could be enrolled was if she signed a declaration that I was unfit to parent. There was no question of us not sending the boys to school, so, in our first month of being in the United States, I was essentially assigned to a mental asylum — on paper, at least.

Our next obstacle was the school itself: after looking through our eldest son's registration package, the school counsellor requested a parents' conference. The outcome of the meeting, which both Tamara and I attended, was the counsellor barring Sebastian from going to school. When we spoke to her about the decision, her response was evasive. To us, it was obvious that homophobia and discrimination played a part, an assumption that was confirmed when our lawyer had a conversation with the school about filing a discrimination suit. After three agonizing days of a young boy asking why he couldn't go to school, we received a phone call saying that the administrative "hiccup" had been cleared.

After the boys got into school and I began my studies at a local community college, we were finally able to start our new life as a family. Tamara and I made friends with people she worked with, who in time became part of our American extended family. Our eldest son, Sebastian, had the hardest time adjusting. His eight years in North Carolina were marred by homophobia at school and his desire to be part of a socially acceptable family. Addison, on the other hand, acclimated in no time. He made friends, settled into school, and had no problem acknowledging his family. In fact, he managed to out us in every English essay he wrote, and by the time he was in middle school, Tamara and I were known by his classmates and other students as Mum One and Mum Two.

Although it may have looked from the outside as if we had settled down permanently, we lived under a constant cloud of uncertainty. As a same-sex couple, Tamara and I were treated as second-class citizens by the US government. As a foreign student, I paid twenty thousand dollars a year in tuition and wasn't allowed to marry without violating the terms of my visa. Neither the state nor the federal government recognized us as a family, which meant that Tamara was considered a single person and taxed accordingly, at a much higher rate. So, as the years passed, we had no way of knowing what the future would hold.

Four years after moving to North Carolina, we realized that our chances of being recognized as a family in the United States were minimal and that we needed to start looking elsewhere. The only countries that would accept us as a family were Canada and the United Kingdom. However, the decision to immigrate to Canada was not an easy one. Tam was devastated that she would have to leave the United States, her family, and her job. We had many fights about leaving, and it made for some hard discussions about our relationship, our family, and what we wanted. In the end, it was the boys' future and our desire to see them grow up in a welcoming environment that caused us to buckle down and start the lengthy application process. We spent months completing paperwork, pooling funds to meet the financial requirements, completing police reports, and, on my part, finally getting a divorce and permission from the boys' father to immigrate. After the application was submitted, we waited anxiously for two years until we were finally accepted by Canada as permanent residents.

On March 7, 2007, we found ourselves walking down a wide hallway from the plane into Toronto's Pearson International Airport toward the new immigrants section. We entered the room, went to the only open counter, and handed our papers to the immigration official, who stamped them, took our photographs, and confirmed our permanent resident status before shuffling us toward customs. The process was so smooth and so quick that it didn't register right away that we had essentially arrived home until Sebastian stopped and, referring to the immigration officer, said, "Mum, I like this country. That was the first time we have ever been called a family."

Walking out of the airport in Toronto that night was for our family the last step on a journey that began when I came out as a lesbian, sixteen years earlier. Leaving our friends who had, by all accounts, become family to us in North Carolina was hard and a reminder of the sacrifices we'd had to make to be accepted as a family. But we are now in our fifth year of living in Ottawa and have become comfortable with our new home.

As we had hoped, Canada has proven a welcoming environment in which two mothers can raise their sons. Sebastian has graduated from university and has come to accept the fact that he has two mums. Since 2010, he has volunteered as a counsellor at Camp Ten Oaks, a summer camp for children of LGBTQ families. His first year was a powerful experience for him and a reminder that he is not the only child that has been or will be conflicted by his upbringing. Addison settled in quickly. He adjusted to his new high school, found a job, and travelled for a year after graduating. He never lost his tendency to out us, and even at Dalhousie University, where he is in his third year, he still manages to mention his lesbian parents in his essays.

Tamara was ultimately able to keep her job in North Carolina. She telecommutes from home, travels back and forth to Africa for work, and makes frequent trips back to North Carolina. The friendships we made while living in the United States remain, and we still look upon the friends we made there as our extended family. For the past three years, all four of us have spent part of our summers there, reacquainting ourselves with a place that was home for eight years.

We have settled in Canada as a family, but a family with a story that many cannot comprehend. It is a story that, for us, has also been a long and complicated journey, athwart with bumps, U-turns, and roadblocks. At times I am still struck by the distance we have travelled and how we have come through relatively unscathed by our experiences. We are like every other family in that we have our ups and downs, battles over parenting and struggles with independence, but we also have a secret bond—the knowledge that we have fought stigma, inequality, the law, and immigration technicalities on two continents so that we could stay together as a family.

Our roots have been turned upside down; we have been transplanted and have learned to survive in spite of everything. Even as social inequalities continue to fall in the United States, and with the demise of the Defense of Marriage Act opening doors for bi-national couples, it is doubtful that we will uproot the family again but, at least for once in our life, we have a choice.

Sebastian's Story

We passed around a little pink piece of paper with a smiley face drawn on it. If you held it in your hands, you could either choose to talk or pass it on. At first, the children were reluctant to speak, and the smiley face moved quickly from hand to hand. Then, one child began to talk. With that one sentence, the floodgates were smashed open by the current of built-up emotion, and all of us— campers and counsellors—found ourselves talking about our experiences of feeling ashamed and alone in a world where the Mom/Dad pairing was idolized and shoved down our throats in everything from television commercials to children's books. As I listened to these kids open their hearts, I felt tears forming and tried not to break down in front of my little campers.

I recall one girl taking the piece of paper and talking about how her parents had divorced when she was five. How she had been angry that her mom loved other women, how she lied when her mom's partner came to pick her up from school, how she felt ashamed and was filled with hatred at the situation her mom had made her live in. That little girl spoke for me. Her experiences were my own, and in twenty-two years of existence, I had never truly accepted them. Yet, here was this brave, amazing, courageous thirteen-year-old girl sharing what I never had the courage to vocalize.

So I broke. The tears came, and I sat in the circle with my head bowed, crying. I was patted on the back, and hugged, but I rebuffed all attempts at comfort. I just sat there listening to my twelve- and thirteen-year-old campers share their stories, and I cried. I cried for years of shame, hatred, and innumerable attempts to be seen as "normal."

That experience, during my first year at Camp Ten Oaks, is the essence of what it's all about. The camp is part of the Ten Oaks Project, an organization that, through its various programs, works to engage and connect the youth of lesbian, gay, bisexual, transsexual, and queer families. Camp Ten Oaks is the only one of its kind in Ontario, and one of only a handful of similar camps in North America.

I found out about the camp through my mother, who was a member of the Ten Oaks board and thought the camp would benefit from someone with my perspective. I was initially hesitant to apply, but after the first couple of days of being involved I knew it was one of the best decisions I'd ever made. At camp, children and staff who identify as LGBTQ or who come from queer families attend for what is on the surface a fun-filled week of activities and sleepovers. What they get is a journey of personal exploration, a validated sense of self, and, above all, a developed awareness of belonging and community.

I will never forget what a good friend of mine said during our end-of-week staff debrief: "It is sad and profoundly ironic that a place as beautiful and right as Camp Ten Oaks must be born from such hatred and ignorance." Born out of the world I tried so hard to be a part of for twenty-two years.

For most of my life I've felt alone, with only my brother to understand how I've felt. My biological parents divorced when I was five and my brother was two. As a five-year-old, my memories of their time together are vague and increasingly harder to recall. However, after the divorce, I remember my mom having a couple of very close female friends—the type who would come over for sleepovers, join us on holidays, and generally just be around. To me, this was normal; it was how things were done and there was nothing more to it. I was vaguely aware of the fact that my mom was attracted to members of her own sex, but mostly I existed in a little bubble of childhood ignorance. My mom's friends were awesome, they gave me toys, and I was well provided for and loved, so there was nothing wrong with the situation as I saw it.

That changed when I turned eleven and moved from Zambia to North Carolina with my brother, my mom, and her now lifelong partner, Tam, and began school in the United States. I remember it slowly dawning on me that I came from vastly different circumstances than my peers, as I heard kids say "that's gay" to refer to something they thought was stupid and calling each other "faggot" as the ultimate insult. Having two moms in North Carolina was not something to advertise. So, I began to hide my home life in an effort to fit in. I started to lie and feel ashamed of having two moms. This negativity ate at me every day. I hated myself for lying, for never speaking up or correcting someone, for even calling things "gay" myself, yet I continued to do it.

When school activities involved talking about our families, I lied and said I had a single mom. My two moms became fused in my head whenever I talked about my family—I would refer to this single super mom with attributes from both of my parents. So, my biological mom became someone who worked at a non-profit doing women's reproductive health research and was simultaneously studying journalism at the University of North Carolina—someone who was Zambian with a distinct colonial English accent, yet was also from Iowa.

In high school, I began to believe that I had a weak, conforming personality because of my constant attempts to hide my home life. Yet I know if I were to go back and do it again, I wouldn't be able to change a thing, not without a place like Camp Ten Oaks for sanctuary every summer. I did what I had to do to be seen as hetero-normative, even though I had a foot in the door of a vastly different world. Only at camp did I finally realize all this, and only there was I finally able to vocalize and then accept it.

There aren't enough adjectives to do the importance of a place like Camp Ten Oaks justice. If I had a place like this growing up, I don't know how I would have turned out, but I do know I would not have been ashamed of my family all those years. I think I would have had a heightened sense of belonging somewhere and wouldn't have felt so alone.

It would be nice to think that things have changed since I was a kid, but today, even in a country like Canada, kids still have to go through the crap I went through. They still have to deal with the undercurrents of homophobia. They still sometimes lie, feel disconnected and exasperated, and ask, "Why me?"

But that one week at Camp Ten Oaks shows them that there is absolutely nothing wrong with their families. It validates everything they fight for and shows them it's okay to be vulnerable, to share and subsequently overcome these feelings of hurt and shame, and, most importantly, to truly know that there are others going through the same thing they go through. I know this because that week has done all these things and more for me.

NOREEN FAGAN's career has spanned many years and continents. She was raised in Zambia, Central Africa, and lived in South Africa, England, and the United States before moving to Ottawa in 2008. She is passionate about human rights and social justice issues, in particular sexual and reproductive rights, HIV/AIDS non-disclosure laws, and sex workers' rights. She has contributed stories to *Indy Week*, *Xtra*, *Open File*, and the *Ottawa Citizen*.

SEBASTIAN CHARGE works at Pressed Cafe in Ottawa. He has done a smattering of writing for Camp Ten Oaks, *Q News*, and the *Queen's Journal*. He also volunteers at the Catholic Immigration Centre, helping newly arrived immigrants settle in Canada. He hopes to attend law school in the fall of 2014.

Piecing My Family Together

JASON DALE

ONE OF THE REASONS my husband, Regan, and I left our jobs in Toronto to move to my hometown of Port Dover, Ontario, was because we wanted to raise kids in a rural community (as we had been) and wanted to be close to our families. But in the midst of buying a home and a dog and getting settled in our new jobs—we're both high school teachers— kids got put on the backburner. Three years later, though, we contacted our local Children's Aid Society (CAS), aware that they were seeking foster and adoptive parents in our area, and began attending the pre-foster and adoption training classes required to start the process. And so began the most incredible, unexpected, heartbreaking, and meaningful adventure of our lives.

In December 2005, after we finished our training, we were assigned a social worker, Laura, who acted as our adoption guide and worked to piece our family together like a puzzle in the years to come. Her first task was a home study. "Are you satisfied with your sex life? What do you love about your partner and what irritates you about him? What did your parents do both right and wrong while raising you? How involved will your extended families be in your potential children's lives? Are you worried about being visible gay parents in this small community? How will you respond when your child one day asks you about his/her birth mother?"

The home study process was sometimes intrusive, but that's as it should be considering the possible outcome and the vulnerable lives at stake. Regan and I simply answered the dozens of questions honestly and without much hesitation. I can assure you, though, we were mighty relieved when the answers we'd provided during our solo discussions with Laura matched up (especially that bit about being sexually satisfied with each other). Awkward or not, we completed the home study process in June 2006, wishing that every parent was vetted so thoroughly before conceiving or raising children.

Four months later and much to our surprise, Laura presented us with the profile and photograph of a four-month-old boy in need of what the CAS dubs a "forever family." She shared all of the information the agency had on the infant and his biological parents, explained the various risks associated with this particular child, and said we had a week to make a decision. We only needed about ten seconds before saying, "Yes!" After Laura left, we wept in each other's arms, stupefied by our good fortune, eager to tell our families and friends that our dream had come true. Seven days later, we met our son for the first time at his wonderfully loving foster home. Regan fed him a bottle and I cradled him to sleep in my arms. It was love at first touch for all three of us.

We brought Rex home for good on November 3. Our families, friends, and colleagues shared in our joy. They deluged our home with literally hundreds of gifts, stopped to hug us on the sidewalk, and offered parenting tips and encouragement to us along the way. Never had I felt so loved, so bolstered by my community, so high on life. I took the nine-month paternity leave we were entitled to and spent my days pushing my boy all over town in the gorgeous navy blue Prince William pram a co-worker had had shipped from England decades before, a family heirloom now on loan to us. Strangers often stopped to peek in at Rex, many sharing their own memories of baby-raising along the way, surprised but supportive upon discovering he had two dads.

Only once did I have a negative encounter, after being set upon by two well-dressed church boys out to "spread the word" and meet their canvassing requirements. They stopped Rex and I, asked if I knew God and whatnot, but refused to listen when I politely told them I wasn't interested. It began raining, so I told them I needed to go, yet they stood in front of the pram, blocking my path, and asked if my wife knew God and why I didn't want my son to live forever. At that point, I was done. I called them on their pushiness and told them to move. "And by the way," I added, "I have a husband, not a wife, and we have this beautiful child, so I don't need what you're selling." That led to some serious facial contortions on their part and pontifications on sin and hell and how terrible my son's life would be with parents like us. With some difficulty, I resisted the urge to strangle them. Those two choirboys have no idea how narrowly they escaped the gay ninja ass-whipping I envisioned as I stomped home in fury.

After the completion of our six-month probationary custody period, the CAS petitioned our local court to arrange Rex's legal adoption ceremony. Although my father had recently been diagnosed with cancer, he insisted on joining everyone assembled at the courthouse to witness the occasion. Judge Edwards gave a moving speech about the unique nature of our adoption, noting that he had never proclaimed the legal adoption of a child to a male couple, praising Regan and I for being teachers and giving back to our communities, concluding, "This is one of my happiest, proudest moments as a judge in Canada. I wish all three of you a wonderful life together." Our families, along with our social worker, Laura, shared hugs, took pictures, and laughed as Judge Edwards allowed Rex to sit in his chair and bang his gavel. We celebrated the fact that Rex was now ours forever.

Two days later, a shocker: Laura came to tell us that a week-old, full biological sister to Rex was in CAS custody, that the agency wanted to keep them together and would support us should we want to pursue her adoption. We agreed right away, the news providing a much-needed lift for the whole family during Dad's chemotherapy, and three weeks later the infant was in our care. Regan and I scrambled to arrange shared paternity leave, me working mornings and him afternoons, passing the "baby baton" over the lunch hour. It was absolute madness, but it was also glorious to watch brother and sister develop a natural bond. Rex doted on her from the start, helping hold her bottles, singing songs to entertain her, and playing with her all day long. Looking back, I realize they were a Dickensian "best of times, worst of times" as I painfully watched my father lose his vitality but revelled in having the "one boy + one girl" perfect family.

Alas, things fell apart on December 20, marked by two phone calls that may haunt me forever. First, my mother called to say Dad had been taken to hospital in critical condition. With Regan at work and no one else to mind the kids, I was frustratingly stuck at home. An hour later, I was watching Rex play and feeding his sister in my arms when the second call came: it was the CAS phoning to say that the judge in our case to formally adopt Rex's sister had instead sided with the biological father's second cousin, awarding her primary custody of the child (our lawyer later explained that Rex, now our legally adopted son, was no longer considered "of his birth families" and therefore the law no longer considered the two children kin, ludicrous as that was). I was told that within two or three hours, a CAS worker would appear at our door to pick up Rex's sister, along with all of her belongings, and deliver her to a complete stranger.

I was literally weak at the knees and dropped to the floor, cradling the baby in my arms, unable to process what had just happened. I wept uncontrollably, confounding Rex and prompting him to come in for a hug in what I am convinced was his effort to console me. Distraught, I phoned Regan's mom, told her what had happened, and asked her to pick him up at school and drive him home, knowing he could never make it safely on his own. Feeling overwhelmed, I called one of my best friends, who rushed over to help with the kids while I tried to compose myself.

Within an hour, Regan and his parents had made it home and we began the awful process of saying goodbye to our girl. Laura and another CAS worker we were close to arrived and hugged us, wept with us, and tried to console us. My friend and Regan's mom put Rex down for his nap and packed up all of his sister's belongings—including lovely not-yet-worn Christmas dresses from my mother and many unwrapped gifts—while we held fast to the girl we had loved as our own. Amid the chaos, my brother called from the hospital in a panic, swearing at me for not being with them as my dad's condition worsened, as yet unaware of the terrible scene playing out in our home. Once I explained things, he offered his sympathy and an apology, and we agreed not to tell Mom since it would only have compounded her grief.

As expected, a CAS worker from another district soon arrived to retrieve the baby, thus beginning the most heart-wrenching minutes of my life to date. We woke Rex up from his nap so he could say goodbye to the sister he loved so much and take some final photos of the two of them together, to be shared when he was old enough to understand. Those assembled at the house carried out boxfuls of belongings, and everyone kissed and hugged the child they had cared about so much, all in tears. And then it was time. I cannot detail the final few minutes Regan and I had with our beloved girl because I want them to remain for us only; besides, I could never find the words . . .

I would say that it was as agonizing as any torture I can imagine except that the next few months—with my father dying in hospital, having to console my mother over the loss of both her husband and the granddaughter she loved but never got to say goodbye to, and Rex searching the house saying, "Sis? Sis?" all his waking hours—were unquestionably more traumatic. I could barely function and took a leave from work. Regan kept our house afloat and cared for Rex like a single parent while I spent my days with my mom and brothers watching my father waste away, my nights spent either weeping or catatonic. Eventually, Regan's love and Rex's joie de vivre reawakened me to life. I privately mourned the twin losses of my father and my daughter but was ultimately able, with time, to be thankful for the husband, son, family, and friends I still had.

Scarred from our experience with Rex's sister, we truly thought we were done with children. We had no contact with the CAS or Laura for ages. We sold our wonderful five-bedroom Edwardian dream home (bought with hopes of filling it with lots of children), the lifeless nursery now a too-painful reminder of the past. Starting over, we bought a small, two-bedroom place four houses down from my mother's on the street I grew up on and readjusted to life, just the three of us.

One year later, Rex, age four, wrote a letter to Santa Claus asking for "slippers, a karaoke machine, and a brother or a sister." Surprisingly, Laura called out of the blue three weeks later, saying it had been a long time and wanting to catch up. She came over and, after a few minutes of small talk, broke into a wide smile, saying, "To be honest, guys, I'm actually here to present to you again, if you're ready. And you may not believe it, but this time there are *two* kids!" Regan and I looked at each other, stunned. The pictures of the boys, ages one and two, melted our hearts immediately. Laura made it clear that these children were already Crown wards, so there would be no legal complications like the last time; essentially, the boys were ours if we wanted them. We said yes within days, having barely slept a wink, dumbstruck by our good fortune, trying to process what this would mean for our lives and wondering how in hell we were going to live as a five-guy family in our two-bedroom house.

We were to meet the foster family a week later, lovely people who had taken great care of the boys. They explained that the one-year-old was always content, loved everyone, and never made strange, but the two-year-old was moodier, very bonded to his foster mom, and often apprehensive around men he didn't know. We were told to prepare for what could be a difficult transition. On our way to meet the boys I felt sick, fearful of being rejected by the older child, already envisioning tears and drama. Instead, the meeting was magical. Coleson, the younger one, was as calm and happy as expected, incredibly walking his very first steps in life toward Regan's ready arms. Seconds later, Grayden came trotting into the room. He and I looked at each other, then he grunted something incomprehensible as I bent down toward him and he moved closer.

Encouraged, I picked him up, he touched my face, and my heart sang. The CAS workers and foster mother were surprised by how easily it went and smiled widely, rightly pleased with themselves for having found the perfect family for these beautiful boys.

On Christmas Day, Rex, along with my mother and Regan's parents, met Gray and Cole for the first time, marking another unforgettable day in our lives. Once again, the transition period from foster home to ours went smoothly, and the boys moved in with us permanently by the end of January. Both Regan and I took leaves from work and spent our days bonding with our boys, helping Rex navigate his feelings of displacement and firming up the emotional foundations of our newly formed quintet. We relied heavily on help from our parents, siblings, and other family and friends who for the third time shared in our unexpected great fortune and showered us with love.

Within months, we knew we wanted a bigger home, but since we loved my old neighbourhood and wanted to remain close to my mom, we opted to renovate instead of moving. As work began, a heat wave struck, rendering us more miserable than the usual hellishness one expects while living in a construction zone would. I bought an inflatable pool, filled it on my mother's front lawn, and lived for a time as gay white trash, flopping about in the water with my screaming, fighting children for all the town to see (and hear), toys strewn all over the place. On one particular day, when no one else was around, I was so desperate for a cold beer that I dried them off, loaded Gray and Cole in the double stroller, clipped the dog to his leash, told Rex to hop on his bike, and off we marched like a mini travelling circus to the Beer Store. I dragged them all inside—yes, even the schnauzer—piled the case atop the stroller, and struggled to get us all back home intact, sweat pouring down my face, kids and dog whining and pulling and yelling and barking. "My God, what have I become?" I asked myself. "Is this really my life, so far removed from the Toronto years?"

Of course, it was, and three years on, I cannot imagine things any other way. I know that while I lived twenty-six years before I met Regan, in the most important ways, my life began with him, and I am grateful for whatever cosmic forces brought us together and gave us these children. And although I have two degrees and spend a good part of my life in a high school, I've realized that my family has taught me more than I could ever hope to learn in a classroom. For example, I now realize that my father was not by nature the sometimes raving lunatic I fondly remember, but rather the antics of his three sons had the power to transform him in an instant, Incredible Hulk–style, and that I am more like him today than I ever could have expected. I've learned that in the grand scheme of things, it doesn't really matter if your child just puked or shat or bled or snotted on your favourite shirt, the leather couch, or the beige carpet, just as I've discovered that trips to Disney World and Dollywood can be just as romantic and awesome as visits to Paris and Bruges. I know not to underestimate the therapeutic, soul-restoring powers of walks and talks with a beloved pet and that hearing your child shriek, "Daddy, this is the best day ever!" can make a grown man tingle inside. I know that CAS workers and foster parents are the unsung heroes of adoption and deserve more recognition for the life-altering work they do on behalf of our nation's neediest children. I know that being a parent is the most difficult and terrifying of jobs but also the most rewarding. Above all else, I know that the adoption process and parenting itself are fraught with unimaginable risks but that the payoffs have given my life its true purpose and filled my heart to bursting.

JASON DALE has taught high school civics and English for fifteen years. In his current role as a student success teacher, he works one on one with at-risk teenagers full of personality and potential. Until now, Jason's only publications have been numerous letters to the editor and open letters to politicians printed in local newspapers. Jason lives in his hometown of Port Dover, Ontario, with his husband, sons, and schnauzer.

Aspiring Lesbian Aunt

ROSEMARY ROWE

I DREADED COMING OUT to my parents and avoided it for years. Unlike many of my fellow queers, I wasn't worried that my folks would reject or judge me. I was worried they'd be REALLY EXCITED and then ask me a lot of personal questions.

My fears were completely founded, by the way. One Christmas night, a little tipsy on Baileys, I finally revealed to my mother that I wasn't a fat loser who couldn't get a boyfriend — I was a fat loser who couldn't get a *girlfriend*. She was thrilled, and within minutes of my confession, she was on the phone with my lesbian aunt, sharing the good news — another gay in the family! And then she asked me a lot of personal questions.

The Baileys helped.

I have always hated sharing personal things with my parents. I simply do not remember a time when I wasn't hiding something from them (or trying to—kids are such terrible liars). I don't know if I was a spy in a previous life—or if perhaps I was a lesbian in a time or place when being queer could get you killed—all I know is that I have always preferred subterfuge to sharing, particularly when it comes to matters of the heart. Or, really, feelings of any kind.

The thing is, my aversion to being honest with my parents has nothing to do with them. My parents aren't crazy evangelicals who sent me to be de-gayed by Exodus. They are very intelligent, liberal-type people who loved and supported me through my sneaky toddler years, my sly elementary years, my emo teen years, and my sullen early twenties, when they offered to pay for my therapy. People would kill to have parents as smart and hip and funny as mine. I am incredibly lucky to have landed with them. Now that I am an adult, I am floored by how awesome they are.

You'd think that having been raised by two such fabulous people I would be eager to follow their example and produce or adopt children of my own. But you'd be so, so wrong. Because the family I have created does not—and likely will not—include kids.

Much as I was loath to confess it to my parents, I was kind of delighted to discover that I was a lesbian. I'd always hoped that there was something genuinely special about me, something out of the mainstream, a kind of difference or distinction that I didn't have to put on. I'd always taken no small amount of pride in bucking trends; realizing that I was a big homo was both a relief and a thrill because it meant that I would have a legitimate excuse not to live a typical "spouse and 2.5 kids" life.

Back when I realized that I did not care for the dick, same-sex marriage wasn't legal in Canada. While I knew that other people found this lack of equal rights unacceptable (weird!), it didn't really bother the young me. If I couldn't legally get married, that meant that no one could make jokes about my not being married without risking a lecture on gay rights. Checkmate!

Similarly, I figured that lesbianism would preclude anyone expecting me to reproduce—because anyone who was keen for me to have kids would inevitably have to utter the word *sperm*, which is gross. I pretty much assumed that as far as "having a family" was concerned, I was off the heterosexual hook and my straight brother would be in charge of delivering the grand-children. Problem solved.

In the early days of my gayness, in the mid-1990s, my conviction that gay people were not expected to have families was backed up by the queer characters in film and on TV. None of these TV gays had families. Instead, it seemed the men were all dying of AIDS and the lesbians . . . ha! That's right, there were no lesbians. Then, later, when shows like *Queer as Folk* came to Canada, it seemed like TV's gay men were all having hot, no-strings-attached, man-on-man sex and the lesbians were having . . . babies. Waaaaait a minute.

Meanwhile, in real life, there began a seemingly never-ending baby boom among my friends and cousins. Some of them were queer, some were straight. Some were married, some were single. Some had fertility issues, some got knocked up by accident. And through it all, my younger brother, my parents' only other hope for grandchildren, kept his mouse in the house.

In the midst of this fictional and real-life baby proliferation, and in light of my brother's extremely responsible approach to birth control, my kid-free resolve started to waiver. I began to feel something I'd managed to stave off most of my life: peer pressure. As I knitted lumpy baby hat after lumpy baby hat for my fecund friends, I started to wonder if I needed to revisit my stance on Mini Me's. Maybe being queer wasn't a good enough excuse to skip having kids. Maybe I *should* have a child. Maybe that was a thing I *had* to do to be a grown up. Or was it?

I mean, I don't *hate* children. When I look at baby pictures of my friends' kids, I do feel slight uterine twinges. Once, long ago, being careful not to pressure me, my mom told me that she totally understood if I wasn't interested in having kids but that she would love to meet "little Rose babies." She looked a little wistful as she said it and that killed me, just a bit. As for my dad—well, he hates kids, but he loved us like crazy, so I wondered if the same thing would happen to me when I met my own biological or adopted child.

After a good deal of soul searching, I decided on a compromise. I didn't want to have kids alone. But if I was lucky enough to meet a soul mate, and my partner in life turned out to be super keen on having children (or already had them), then I would get on board. Not reluctantly, like a douche, but wholeheartedly. I would do it. I would totally do it. I would SO do it.

Then I met Kate.

Kate is very different than I am. I am generally uncertain about things and weirdly miserly with my time and energy. Kate is very confident and successful and generous with her time and ideas. I like to stay indoors and watch TV; Kate likes to go places and do stuff and learn new things. I am wildly impatient and freak out when things don't go my way. Yeah, I'm a real catch. Fortunately, Kate is very patient and good at teaching people new things without making them feel like an idiot.

I knew when I met her that Kate was the kind of person who would be a good parent. And if I was like Kate, I would probably *want* to have kids. And with someone as capable as Kate at the helm, I thought, surely my own fears and objections to having kids would evaporate. I put together a list of good reasons to have children, just in case. Because when Kate inevitably brought up wanting kids, I wanted her to feel supported and never to leave me.

Reasons to have kids:

My parents would be fantastic grandparents; plus, all of their siblings are grandparents and sometimes I feel sad that they aren't having that experience too.

Any child we have will, I hope, feel obligated enough by our years of parental sacrifice to visit me and Kate in the raisin ranch when we are elderly and check us for bedsores.

Help? With . . . chores? I don't know, I'm reaching here.

A few weeks after we met, I took Kate to my friend Julia's wedding. We were seated at a table with Julia's cousin and her little baby. She offered to let us hold the baby and Kate and I declined—in stereo. Then, later in the evening, the baby managed to undo the ties of her mom's halter dress, threatening to expose her mother's ample bosom. We all rolled into action: Kate grabbed the baby, Julia's cousin clutched her own bosom, and I jumped up to help her tie her top back on. I looked over at Kate, who was holding the baby out in front of her like it might explode. The baby was screaming like the Nazgûl, and Kate, laughing so hard she was crying, leaned over and shouted, "CHILDREN LOVE ME!"

As you can imagine, I fell hopelessly in love with her.

Three years later, I, the person who never wanted to be a smug married person, proposed to Kate via an engraving on the back of a new video iPod. Before she said yes, she asked, through tears, if the iPod was the eighty gigabyte (it was). Nerd love! The next year, we got gay married, surrounded by our loved ones. And once we had made that lifelong commitment to love and cherish each other, all that was missing was . . . nothing! Nothing was missing. We, along with Emmy Lou, the rescue Shar-Pei we adopted, made a complete unit. A fat, happy, fuzzy family.

As it turns out, this feeling of completeness is very good. Because, as it turns out, my list of reasons *not* to have kids is a lot longer and more inspired than my list of reasons *to* have kids.

Reasons not to have kids:

I don't like them.

They require a lot of attention.

They are unpredictable and non-verbal for an extended period.

They make me want to create a device that modulates the pitch of their voices so that their screaming will become more pleasing to me.

I might fuck them up.

They might put strychnine in the well.

I hated my parents with a fiery passion when I was a kid and I don't ever want to inflict that pain on another human or have it inflicted on me.

Seriously . . . I was such a jerk as a kid. Oh, I didn't kill anyone or shoplift like an idiot, but I was a selfish, self-absorbed, compassionless twat until my late teens. I honestly don't know how my parents made it through, and here's the thing—there is *nothing* that they could have done to make me change my behaviour or confide in them. They did their best, but I was the living worst.

I read an article recently about a woman whose mentally ill son threatens her life so often that her other kids have a "safety plan" where they run and lock themselves in the car and call 911. After reading it, I said to Kate, "If that was my kid, I'm sorry, but he would be in an institution *immediately.*"

I don't want to have kids.

$$\mathcal{Q} \quad \mathcal{Q} \quad \mathcal{Q}$$

Ultimately, the best reason not to have kids is not wanting to have kids. People who don't want kids should not have them. Now that I've married a woman who also does not care for children, I realize how totally relieved I am that I will not have to do this. Honestly, I feel like I experience as much as I want to of parenthood by having a dog. Let's be clear — I'm not comparing having a dog to having a child. Why would I do that? The whole point of having a dog is that a dog is nothing like having a child.

Our dog is pretty much the anti-child. In fact, she's practically the anti-dog. She's more like a suspicious cat, really, who has the decency to shit outdoors instead of in a box. Since we adopted her from the rescue shelter, we have seen Emmy Lou through some crazy phases, such as her restless toddler years, where she only slept for sixteen hours a day instead of twenty; her stubborn teen years, where she would practise selective hearing at the off-leash park and also started smoking; and her crabby senior years, when she likes to her pull her panties up real high and will only go on a walk if she smells a cat in the direction she'd like to go.

When Emmy Lou leaves us, I imagine we will rescue another dog and begin the cycle again. Our wrinkly dogs will never be able to take care of us in our old age . . . but that's what retirement savings and Japanese robots are for. Who knows, maybe we'll sponsor some young doctor's tuition through her years of medical school in return for a weekly bedsore check in our old age. Or maybe my goddamn brother will finally sire me a niece. I think I would make a really hilarious aunt.

I still occasionally have moments of parental inclination. For example, lately I have felt really inspired by our friends and family who've adopted kids from other countries or right here at home — older kids, kids with special needs, any kid who needs a home. I think those parents (or, really, all parents) are fucking heroes. I am in awe of them. I'm so thankful that they exist and that they have that child-raising drive I seem to lack. And I think, Heeeey! Maybe we could do that too!

That's when I have to remind myself to check out my list again. Because when it comes down to it, while I sometimes fantasize about being the ultimate parent, I don't actually want to *be* a mom — I just want to play one on TV.

ROSEMARY ROWE is a Vancouver-based playwright and blogger. Recently, her cabaret piece *Anne and Diana Were TOTALLY DOING IT* was published in *Queering the Way: The Loud & Queer Anthology*, and her new play, *Camp Victoria*, debuts at Calgary's Lunchbox Theatre in 2014. Rose's blog, creampuffrevolution.com, landed her a spot as a national finalist on CBC's Canada Writes—on the same day as her wedding. She did not win on the radio . . . but she did win at love.

A History of Peregrination

DANNY GLENWRIGHT

"WHERE DID YOU LEARN to speak English so well?"

That was the first thing he ever said to me. It wasn't meant as a pickup line—it was more of a question, the type one might ask a gay couple at a Jehovah's Witnesses service. What are you doing here? How does this *work*, exactly?

He thought I was Brazilian (which could have passed for a pickup line).

I laughed, replying that English was my first, and only, language. Then I noticed his eyes—almond-shaped and complaisant—and guessed he was West African. A few years earlier, I'd lived in Freetown, so I was somewhat practised at recognizing people from that part of the world. (His family is from southeastern Ghana, I would later find out.) I go weak-kneed for African men; it's absolutely hopeless. Ten minutes before I'd met him, I was on the dance floor snogging another black man, exploring his mouth with my tongue. It had been a long time, and I was in heat—carnal and on the prowl.

We were in Rio de Janeiro, in the queue for the bathroom at a moist, heady gay club called The Week. I had flown in two days before from the West Bank, where I'd been living for fifteen months, working in Bethlehem on a human rights campaign. It had been almost as many months since I'd had sex; I had been forced back into the closet by local customs, cloistered away in the cradle of Jesus. I spent my nights in a lonely apartment with a remarkable view of an ugly illegal Israeli settlement, my only succor a weekly date with a pack of Marlborough Lights, a bottle of cheap red wine, and seancody.com.

I remember introducing him to my Brazilian friend Carlos and telling him I was Canadian. We were both in Brazil on holiday: I was visiting friends in Sao Paulo and the Amazon, while he'd been at a psychology conference in Buenos Aires and taken a few extra days to explore the country. We had that "what a small world" conversation after he told me he lived in Toronto, which was my home base when I wasn't living abroad. He'd overheard mine and Carlos's chatter and was excited to find English speakers in the topless sea of *bom dia* and *tudo bem*. We exchanged a few more pleasantries and then said goodbye, cool to meet you, see you on the dance floor maybe.

I can't recall what happened next. I was likely enticed by

the cajoling beats of Robin S. or the promise of a cold Skol beer. I was intoxicated and the club had a slightly subaqueous feel, which may account for why my memories of that night have slowly washed away, like sand from under one's toes after a day on Ipanema. The details of our most life-changing moments are often strangely tenuous.

Years later, he and I still tell different stories about how it happened. He says I found him a while later on the dance floor, approaching with a story about needing him to dance with me because some *Carioca* was following me. I can't imagine why that would've bothered me. If it did occur that way, I'm sure it was my version of the movie-theatre-yawn-and-stretch move, my arms soon over his shoulders. I, on the other hand, remember him finding me at the bar. I thought he'd sought me out, wanting to find out more about what had brought me to Brazil.

However it happened, we ended up at the same place. We were dancing when he stopped and looked straight at me. "You have nice lips," he said. "Well, then, you'd better kiss them," I replied. The kiss was brief, but it worked. I met many men that first night of freedom from the chaste Levant, but I didn't sleep with any of them. Instead, I made plans to take my Canadian boy on a proper date the next time I was in Toronto. He went home, Carlos and I danced; I was in glorious Rio.

🐒 🐒 🐒

Three months later, we were two bottles in on a Toronto patio, and he had me at nomenclature. It was the first time I'd ever known anyone to use the word — successfully! — in a sentence. And he just kept going, without even a pause to digest this sirloin vocabulary selection, rambling about whatever it was we'd been discussing. But I'd stopped listening. I was already falling in love.

It was the date I'd promised him in Rio, our first. He was late, but he was also urbane, inquisitive, and beautiful. For all his impressive language, he also possessed a West African lassitude, an appealing moderation in his words, outlook, and movements. I wanted to be around him more; I wanted to hear him speak to me, all the time. In those first months I would ring his cell phone even when I knew he wasn't around to answer, just to listen to his voicemail message.

He later told me he'd come to that first meeting only to follow through with his South American promise. He was dating someone else; it was to be a quick dinner and then goodbye. I guess I also sucked him in. He loves my arrant opinionating, my floppy hair, and my unapologetic left-wing politics. And we both had travel behind us, an essential history of peregrination. In the years prior to meeting him I'd been Huckleberry Finning my way around Africa and the Middle East. I'd lived in five countries in as many years. One psychologist had told me I was running away from intimacy, too frightened to repeat the mistakes of my parents, using travel like tae kwon do.

But he had travelled too and understood its protective layers and my addiction to escape. He'd been raised by his mother in Ghana, northern Manitoba, and Pakistan. I knew his traditional food; he knew my unresolved Oedipal conflicts. He was the first person who ever made me want to slow down my life, which until then had been like a BBC weather report, the kind where the meteorologist has two minutes to get from

Bangalore to Santiago, a race repeated at the end of every broadcast; I'm sure each person watching yearns for just a moment's pause over his Alberta clipper. He allowed me to see that I longed to stay in one place and see the weather through all four seasons, with one person. Being with him, it was as if I was slowly uncovering the use of something I'd been lugging around for years.

Fear of sexual intimacy and commitment is nothing special; therapists rely on both to pay the bills. I don't know the complicated recipe that created these fears in me, but for years they were constantly present, waiting for me to decide to vanquish them. With friends I've always been gregarious, outspoken, and, yes, quite intimate. A connector, a little hot sauce with every meal. Those who have known me a long time often joke, "Who *isn't* your best friend?"

And while it's true that I'm flush with friends, relationships were for a long time out of reach. At fifteen, I knew I liked men; by seventeen, I had told all my friends I was gay, but by twenty-one, I had still not had gay sex. And there were opportunities. I look back now with frustration at how many I missed. I moved out on my own when I was sixteen and spent several years working in restaurants by day and conquering the rave scene in my hometown of Winnipeg by night. I was popular and surrounded with gay men, yet I erected invisible obstacles that prevented me from being the sexually healthy gay man I could have been. I recall telling friends that I preferred to spend time focusing on my social life rather than sexual relationships. But there's no good reason I couldn't have had both.

So I found the easiest answer and blamed my surroundings, my city. I left Winnipeg for the first time at twenty and headed to Europe like so many confused teenagers before me. I was back a year later and nowhere closer to contentment. I fled again, this time to Toronto. It was a pattern I repeated for many years.

But it wasn't only a way to escape — I found great joy in those years of travel and in human rights journalism. I'd wanted to see the world ever since I was quite young. Even as a kid, I was at ease spending time alone. I took up reading earlier than most children my age and remember plowing through James Michener and Colleen McCullough in Grade 4 when the rest of my classmates were wrestling with Judy Blume. And while they rode bikes and played with G. I. Joe, I read newspapers and kept manila folders filled with clippings documenting provincial and federal elections.

When I eventually realized my goals and ended up on far-flung adventures of my own, I revelled in my ability to connect with others and help with their issues. I also tackled some of my own. I found moments of love and plenty of sex. I opened up with the help of liquor, which became a *sine qua non* in my explorations of intimacy. It would have been enough, but then I found something better.

☙ ☙ ☙

The first several months of our relationship proved revelatory. They were spent in Toronto, but my new man was a man of the world. We circled the globe without leaving the neighbourhood. He shopped at T&T, an Asian supermarket, and created Thai dishes with ingredients only he could pronounce. He drank chilled green tea and ordered Chinese takeout in Mandarin, a language he'd picked up during five years living in Taiwan. He rose before me on Sundays and snuck out to a Sri Lankan bakery in Cabbagetown, returning with cheese Danishes and strong black coffee.

While I'll always be bibulous, he was the first man who made me comfortable enough to do away with my vestigial get-drunk-before-sex ritual. I stopped requiring alcoholic protection and I changed course, allowing a new, and life-changing, experience that didn't involve boarding a plane.

In a few short weeks we had history, but our pause in Toronto proved to be a metaphorical one; we never saw the same four seasons together that first year. We had expedited our relationship, but circumstance and prior commitments meant it had to be built over distance. Certainty in each other and Skype sex were the adhesives that bound us in that first year. Four months in and I had already left Toronto for a job in Rwanda. I phoned him one day from a building site outside Kigali, where I was working with a group that had spent the day constructing a school for the local kids. A toddler from the village discovered me after I snuck behind a hut to phone him. She sat silently on my lap, stroking my blond arm hair while I chatted with my new Canadian boyfriend. He asked me to snap her picture so I could show him when I got home. He was the first lover who had ever understood what I did and why I needed to do it. He would have felt comfortable there beside me.

I thought of George W. Bush glad-handing in Haiti after

the 2010 earthquake, almost reflexively wiping the imagined Haitian cooties from his fraudulent hand all over Bill Clinton's sweaty shirt. So many people are like politicians—pretending in order to profit, isolated in an open world. I'd discovered someone who was not like that—someone who made it easy to discard the hang-ups I'd been holding on to for too long.

I returned smiling to the group and helped carry large foundation boulders for the school while daydreaming about my boyfriend's naked body, in a country where the type of sex we have is illegal.

෴ ෴ ෴

It was fortunate that I managed to scrape off the last barnacles of self-doubt and commitment-phobia during those first months of our relationship because we'd soon be wrestling with larger challenges, both imagined and real.

While recent census data from Canada and the United States have shown an increase in both same-sex and inter-racial couples (as well as same-sex interracial couples), we were initially acutely aware of our status as both a gay and mixed couple—mostly because we spent so much time outside North America.

Whenever I'm concerned about being caught out in places where my sexuality is seen as something depraved or shameful, there is always one question that runs through my mind: *Do you think people can tell?* This anxiety is exacerbated when I'm travelling with a same-sex partner. *Do they know what we just got up to in the hotel room?* Even fully clothed and a foot apart, strolling in public, each glance or stare makes me feel as naked as Goya's *Maja*. But it's like so many things in life that occur in the clandestine world of the mind: why would they know? And really, who cares if they do?

So picture it: Venice, moments after I proposed on a gondola (he said yes!). We had stopped for a celebratory drink at an outdoor café near Campo San Zaccaria and were hopelessly giddy. We sat in the sun, too nervous to hold hands across the table, but our body language behaved as if manipulated by electricity. Our waiter eventually turned up, ornery and brusque. He took stock of the situation, glancing at both of us in turn. My new fiancé hesitated over the Italian menu, unsure of what to order. "What cocktails do you have?" he asked, hoping the waiter could understand some English.

"Bevanda?" I tried in my best Italian.

The grumpy older man, who behaved as if it was his first day juggling a section filled with ignorant tourists (I'd bet a wad of euros it wasn't), rolled his eyes and tsked.

"Negroni, Americano," he huffed back.

At this, my sweetheart jumped to his feet, threw down his menu, and stormed away.

He turned back. "Are you coming?" I winced at the waiter, managing to murmur a hasty "grazie mille," before catching up with my angry companion.

"I can't believe it, the racist asshole," he said, which is when, for me, the penny dropped.

I had been living in Italy for several months, completing a master's degree at a university outside Milan. By that time I was very familiar with Italy's potent Campari-based cocktails, including those the waiter had suggested. My new fiancé, who had only arrived a few days prior to our Venetian weekend, was not. To him, those two words spit contemptibly at us meant very different things.

I explained. We laughed and stopped at another café. I had a delightful Negroni while he had his first Americano.

My wanderlust next took us to Johannesburg, just a few days after we'd exchanged vows. A new job for me, our first home together, and a job hunt for my new—and brave—husband. It was a win-win from my perspective: if the relationship went out the window, at least I was abroad and living my dream. We fought often in those first months; our love felt strong, but our union was like an infant's fontanelle, sensitive and still under construction.

I became frustrated when he would arrive home angry or crestfallen. He would treat me to a deluge of stories about how he'd been mistreated by black South Africans he suspected were homophobic or prejudiced. He was unhappy, questioning our decision to move. I remember accusing him of paranoia and hypersensitivity. "It's all in your head," I'd say.

I took a reluctant pause then to digest the great speed with which I'd pulled myself away from a life of solitary freedom to one of domestic bridge-building. I'd decided that my own life would no longer be enough for me. But was I wrong? My own internal fissures reopened in those months, sowing dangerous Monsanto seeds of doubt.

Then, one day he called me at work from a police station. He'd been pulled over by bored police officers on his way to a job interview, a job we desperately needed him to get because we were running low on funds. The officers didn't believe his Canadian passport was genuine, nor did they recognize his international driver's licence or the car's registration. My husband was shaken at the time, worried to mention that it was his male spouse's car. He hesitated, responded at first with ambiguity, but eventually admitted our relationship, showed the officer a photo of us, and ended up in police custody. He also missed the job interview.

It was an extreme example of the type of discrimination he'd been experiencing, which I had discredited. The legacy of apartheid is rapacious and demoralizing and also something of an enigma for outsiders. We were prepared for South Africans to take issue with our sexuality, but we didn't foresee that the bigger obstacle would be skin colour: both the interracial nature of our relationship and my husband's black skin and foreign accent.

Despite the fact that in a few months' time he was making more money than me, black bank managers repeatedly refused him when he tried to open a South African account. In one instance, the very same bank manager who'd rubber-stamped my new account denied my husband the same service, even though he was in possession of the identical documentation that had worked for me. The bank eventually relented, but while I was given a credit card with a huge limit and "elite" banking status (which meant I had the bank manager's mobile phone number and a negotiable overdraft), he was only approved for a basic account and the pleb card—no credit, no overdraft.

I apologized then for doubting what he'd been going

through. Being wrong in a relationship is a miraculous thing—frustrating in the moment, but in the grand scheme, a revelation. You give something each time you're wrong and traversing the fallout means growth, that Oprah buzzword that rings true if you listen. I acknowledged to my husband that it hadn't worked out as flawlessly as in my Rwandan daydreams.

And so we did what Boer strangers in South Africa did many decades ago: we built a *laager*. In those bloody colonial days, the circling of wagons helped ward off wild animals and (rightfully) angry natives. Ours was a shield against those outside our electric fence who destroyed our spirits with modern South Africa's arbitrary corruption and its residue of oppression—those who waved my white face through police roadblocks but arrested my black husband, those who glowered at him when he was unable to speak their language, and those who refused to provide services unless we passed along a cash bribe.

In many ways, we learned to love Jozi's knottiness. Over the years, and even after moving to our current home in Toronto, we've continued adding to our *laager*, yet are always cautious of its fragility—aware that fortifications can be broken by something as capricious as a sneeze. Either way, after that first year living together we were no longer operating from two different systems. I should really send thank-you cards to all those who wronged us, including myself. We're moving forward, in Canada, South Africa, or wherever we take ourselves. I can no longer imagine doing any of it alone.

DANNY GLENWRIGHT is the managing editor of *Xtra* newspaper in Toronto. He has a background in human rights journalism and media training and was previously the editor of the Gender Links Opinion and Commentary news service in South Africa and a regular contributor to South Africa's *Mail & Guardian*. He has also worked in Sierra Leone, Palestine, Namibia, the United Kingdom, and Rwanda. He is the co-author of the *Southern Africa Gender and Media Progress Study* and the co-editor of the *Gender and Media Diversity Journal: Gender, Popular Culture and Media Freedom*.

To Carry My Family in My Imperfect Head

ARLEEN PARÉ

TWO YEARS AGO, *Leaving Now* was published — I had been writing it for ten years. *Leaving Now* is a novel that's not exactly fiction: it's a fairy tale that breaks traditional rules, a memoir that includes poetry and events of questionable veracity. I wrote it as an apologia, an explanation to my two children about what I had done thirty years ago that derailed their perfectly ordinary, almost perfect lives. It is an apology to them.

When I left home on Saturday, June 28, 1980, the first day of summer vacation, I was thirty-four years old, old enough to leave home. But the home I was leaving was not the home of my parents: it was the home of my husband and my two sons and me, a unit of almost thirteen years. We got along. We liked one another—most of the time. We were an ideal sort of family: a mother, a father, two children, and one small silver schnauzer. We were the right number, the right types of individuals filling each familial category with no complicated blending, no two or three mothers, no extra children, no cats, no ferrets, no boa constrictors. The father was a doctor, which was ideal, in that Hollywood kind of way. The mother was a social worker, who worked part-time out of the house, in that *Chatelaine* magazine perfect kind of way. She drove her two boys to soccer games, made well-balanced dinners, and read the boys stories at night. Ideal. They lived in a Vancouver bungalow with a standard measure of harmony—nothing cloying, nothing vicious.

But we are goaded by perfection, according to British philosopher Kenneth Burke. This means we're almost always afraid of being less than ideal. This means we are almost always afraid. Contrary to my description of my perfect family of four, it was, of course, less than ideal, not because the two children were not exemplary, nor because the father was not kind, nor because the mother didn't love them all very much. It was not ideal because the ideal does not exist in real life. It exists only in our minds.

Things have changed since 1980. Ideals have changed too, although in some ways, our minds carry on. Things had already started to change in the mid-1960s. The pill, women's liberation, Black Power, gay pride, for instance. The concept of the standard ideal had begun to unravel. Maybe this has been true throughout history; there are always some groups interested in change. Maybe there have always been ways of questioning ideals and then slightly shifting them. I had started to question the entire social status quo, the fabric of my world, as early as 1970, two years after I was married and had my first child. I had joined a consciousness-raising group that year. I became a woman's libber, as they once referred to women interested in our own freedom—a feminist, as we now say. We wanted what men considered their birthright. Nine years later, following that same trajectory, and suddenly, without intention, falling head over heels in love with a woman, I became a lesbian.

That was the summer of 1979. Through the fall, I spent night after night trying to solve the conundrum: how to maintain a sense of family togetherness but move on into my new lesbian life. In September, I told my husband. He was ready to live with the idea that I was having an affair with a woman—he thought. I told my two children, who found it disturbing at the time, but it didn't seem to upset their day-to-day lives, as far as I could tell. I spent the hour before I fell asleep trying to come up with a logistical arrangement that kept the family together but not *together*. But I found no solution. I could not think my way out of this dilemma. We lived together, day by day, as if things were the same, but things were not the same. It became harder and harder for my husband and I to talk about ordinary things—most topics were mined with pain.

This was less than ideal. That is to say, it was less than ideal as far as maintaining an intact, fully functioning, standard family. It was much less than ideal for my husband, though if I had fallen in love with another man, that, too, would have been imperfect. It was not perfect for the children; they were used to having two parents of different genders, used to *us*. And because it was upsetting for all of us, the schnauzer, as though a silver lightning rod, got a rash, started to lose its thick silver coat, and became slightly untrained, which is not ideal in a pet. We were all wrecks. To be fair, we were all under forty and very unused to the tectonic shifts of life.

Finally, the pain of living together without real togetherness became unbearable. In the spring of 1980 I decided I had to leave. No one else was going to leave, and staying in one home left my husband and me drained and unhappy. I believed our unhappiness was bad for the kids. Who knows? Although a few family members knew about my "affair," most did not. None of our mutual friends knew. Everyone still thought we were an ideal couple. And really, this state of affairs could no longer be considered a single "affair"; I now called myself a lesbian, and despite former familial "perfection" and pursuits thereof, I was not coming back. Though I had tried to find the perfect solution, once the ideal code had been broken, the family was flawed. It happens all the time.

I found a room to rent on Crown Street about twenty blocks away and moved in on June 28, 1980. It was a horrible day. My twelve-year-old son had put on weight over the winter, cushioning himself, I suppose, against the uncertainty of the family's direction. On the day I moved out, my ten-year-old son ran away for an hour. When he reappeared, we felt we had done enough for the day, but still I had to leave them. It was just after noon when I left. I was in a state of suspended animation, I think. The sky was overcast, the day windless as I drove away down the lane. That evening, their father took the boys to see *Peter Pan* at a theatre on Main Street. I don't know how my boys got to sleep without me tucking them in. Maybe they didn't sleep all that night long. I think it could have been then that I began *Leaving Now*. Although my conundrum was solved, it was not solved satisfactorily. This is the nature of the less than ideal, I suppose, and it led to guilt and unrest — to the book, and to the eventual apology.

Their father and I moved back and forth, into and out of the main house where the boys continued to reside, every two weeks for three years. I think at the time, this arrangement was called "the bird nest." I had read about the arrangement and thought it could work for us. The boys were able to stay in their same school and after classes and on weekends they could race around the same old neighbourhood with their same friends. We had agreed to have family meetings regularly. It should have been ideal. But it wasn't. I always felt bad, guilty for bringing this change into all of our lives. Though I tried to call family meetings, we weren't able to keep up with them on a regular basis. I think we only met twice, maybe three times.

Then, after three years, the house started to look rundown without one consistent in-house parent to properly oversee the cleaning, maintenance, and repairs, to infuse the rooms with cheer on a regular personal basis. I thought my oldest child's friends (he was almost fifteen by then) weren't coming around the house as much, and I thought maybe I, their lesbian mother, had become a detriment to their social lives. I think their father's new girlfriend wanted them to have their own home, to become the boys' mother. I thought teenaged boys might need a father more than a mother, need him more than me. So, after three years, an accumulation of such issues persuaded me to move out of the bird nest. I became more of a weekend parent, even though I was more their emotional parent. We all had to steel ourselves once again.

After that, I think I began to carry my family more internally, in my heart and my head, given that I had moved my family, the part I still belonged to, out of its original home. Despite this external change, my family remained firmly housed in my mind. Although I saw the boys often, I no longer saw them for everyday meals or to help them with homework or to chat for ten minutes after school. Maybe few other mothers were chatting with their teenaged boys for ten minutes after school; I don't know. They were adolescents by then and busy shaping their own independence. All that was thirty years ago, but the foundation for subsequent unhappiness had been set: I could not shake my sense of unbelonging and guilt. Many mothers will tell you about their guilt. Guilt and motherhood are two sides of one coin in some way; mothers can never be perfect, can never do enough. Life itself is too imperfect—no mother can make up for that.

The boys grew up and became decent, considerate men. They have good jobs. They found partners they will likely spend the rest of their lives with. One has two sons himself, my two grandsons, who are almost the ages of my sons when I first left. My sons are almost perfect even without perfect pasts. For years I blamed myself for anything that hurt them in their lives, for whatever went wrong. Not in any dramatic, chest-pounding way—just to myself, like small drops of acid. This is what can happen. I had believed they were entitled to ideal childhoods. I believed, as so many do, that no mother should leave her children. Nonetheless, I left. Even now, I can't imagine how I did it, how I made it okay enough that I could leave at all. But there is no perfection, and in the end, they made things work out for themselves. They wanted good lives by and large. They have even said that they were fortunate to have a lesbian mother, that they would not now be so open or flexible, so willing to try to understand difference, if they had carried on with their ordinary, almost perfect childhoods. They think they are lucky. I think they are very positive young men.

I maintained decent relationships with my former husband and his family. My long-term lesbian partner, the one I married three years ago, supported me in maintaining all my familial ties. Few people blamed me. Nonetheless, although I would not change being a lesbian for anything, I blamed myself for leaving the family to imperfection and sadness.

In the end, I had to write an official apology—an explanation to myself and to my boys. It took ten painful years. I remembered what I could and imagined whatever the emotional truth of the matter could bear. This is my book. Even if it had never been published, after my sons had read it, I began to feel better. I think they felt better too. That's what an apology does: it makes everyone feel better, perfect or not. I was able to rejoin my family, outside my head, and bring the three of us back together in a real way, in the real, not ideal, world.

ARLEEN PARÉ is a Victoria poet and novelist with an MFA in creative writing from the University of Victoria. Her first publication, *Paper Trail*, was nominated for the BC Book Prizes' Dorothy Livesay Poetry Prize and won the Victoria Butler Book Prize in 2008. Her second novel, *Leaving Now*, was released in 2012 by Caitlin Press. She has published work in literary journals such as *CV II*, *Geist*, and the *Malahat Review*, as well as in numerous anthologies, including *Walk Myself Home*. Her third book, a collection of poetry, *Lake of Two Mountains*, is forthcoming from Brick Books in April 2014.

Wife

KATE BARKER

"ARE YOU KATE BARKER'S wife?" The question took Kim by surprise. It was toward the end of another art show where I had been of little use, mired in the absurdity of being a middle-aged graduate student. The woman stood in front of Kim's pottery booth, smiling, with her husband and kids lingering in the background. The question made Kim inordinately happy.

"Yes," she said. "Yes, I am."

No one had ever asked us that before.

We've been together a long time—nearly twenty years. Ten years ago, I would have made a crack about lesbian relationships being measured in roughly equivalent dog years. Now, I just think it's unusual for anyone to be happily married for more than five minutes.

And yet, I choke on the word *wife*. Kim has always been my partner, even after we nipped down to Toronto City Hall on the quiet in July 2003 to say "I do" before a justice of the peace. There was no wedding; it was a private affair. We just wanted to protect our rights, to make them ironclad. No big deal, we said. We'd already been living together for six years. It didn't change anything. We weren't getting married for the steak knives, we joked, even though that's exactly what my parents gave us in the end. We marked our ceremony on the calendar as though it were a double dental appointment. Friday, 3 PM: get married; Saturday 6 AM: set up for an art show. We hadn't even thought about pictures. Thankfully, one of our witnesses had, so today there is at least the requisite photo on the mantel of our "big day."

We were probably the JP's first lesbian couple. She was chuffed to be officiating, and a little nervous, choosing gender non-specific and secular references to love and unity and in the process mistaking George Eliot for a man, which endeared her to us both. Clearly, she did something right, as Kim and I surprised ourselves by crying through much of the ceremony. We hadn't expected that: to be so shaken by the power of ritual, by saying the words out loud to each other. The next day, in one instant, the reasons for getting married sharpened for me into the hard glint of a knife edge. Driving on my way to meet Kim, a car crash unfurled before me in the cartoon slow-motion and Dolby surround-sound of real-time terror — screaming tires and steel crunching through steel. Even then, when I thought I was about to make her a widow, I didn't think of Kim as my *wife*.

My reticence to use the word is curious. Why do I find it

so cringe-inducing? It has something to do with a life spent on the outside. As a lesbian, I am convinced, since becoming a zygote, I'm used to not fitting in completely. All of a sudden, Kim and I could become Mrs. and Mrs. Beaver Cleaver. It just felt strange. But clearly *wife* best encapsulates all that we are to each other. "It's not cancer," Kim's calm, low voice coming to me before I could worry out the question, or even fully open my eyes, emerging from a hot morphine haze after abdominal surgery. Or "It's my father," her voice dead on the phone, and I knew in a physical chill through my own body that his heart was failing. But a marriage isn't the sum of its most dramatic moments. It's mainly all those little in between parts that matter. Ours has even survived that universal marriage-busting stress, gay or straight—home renovation. In our case, an endless, largely self-conducted, and still ongoing refurbishment to the hundred-year-old house that's been our leaky, drafty, never-finished but much-loved home for most of our marriage. That's saying something. A lot of couples blow apart before the first layer of grimy old brick dust settles.

What's our secret? We've been asked this by many friends over the years and usually reply with as much insight as a Hallmark card: "We don't take each other for granted." But that's a lie. I take her for granted every time I leave a trail of toast crumbs from the kitchen to the TV half an hour after she's vacuumed. Couples take advantage of each other all the time. It's what couples do. Our secret, if we have one, is easier to explain by looking at the underbelly of our relationship, at the soft, podgy, pale bits we don't like to expose to the light. If you really want to pinpoint what works, you have to consider what happens when it all goes to hell. For us, that occurs the second we stop talking to each other. Note I said talk, not *process* — that feminist-therapist doublespeak that only makes me think of Kraft singles and leaves a similar plastic taste in my mouth. What's truly scary is just how quickly it can all go pear-shaped when we fall quiet. That shouldn't be surprising — scrambling communications is a surefire strategy to befuddle the enemy in war. But once we break through our little domes of silence and repair the connection, the largely misconstrued petty hurts we'd been privately nursing against each other melt away.

Kim and I also share a weird bond. I don't believe in God or fate or even blind luck, but I do believe I will always be able to find her, wherever she is in time and space — and I'm directionally deficient. I get lost everywhere, and maps and GPS only confuse me more. But I can always find Kim. I once honed in on her in a strange city when we had no plans to meet but were both suddenly desperate to be together. Some might think that's a little creepy. I think of it as a quantum entanglement.

And we laugh together. A lot. An up-ended paint can or crown moulding installed ass-backwards, even after carefully measuring twice and cutting once, will produce this first response: "Silly bitch." We put up with each other's obsessions and foibles with good grace. Like my running craze, which I foisted upon Kim a few years ago, despite a chunky physicality that makes me more water buffalo than gazelle. My insane determination to train for a fifty-kilometre trail race, having taken up running again after a twenty-plus-year hiatus, was met with neither derision nor snide remarks but rather, after seeing how much it meant to me, and knowing my peculiar determination once any task is set, with a special Christmas present. In spite of her aesthetic ideal of an uncluttered space, Kim bought me the ultimate space-hog—a treadmill. And when, one week before Christmas, on the very first day of training for said ultra, I went out on a ten-kilometre jaunt and sustained a hip stress fracture, she didn't complain. Not even when that goddamned treadmill remained boxed, blocking up our hall for the next nine months because I couldn't place any weight on my injured leg to help schlep it up the stairs. There was no "I told you so." Instead, there she was, seventeen months after the injury, clapping as I came in next to last in a twenty-five-kilometre trail race.

When threatened, we close ranks—protect the core. Through a friend's suicide, watching as our parents age and sicken—we herd instinctively into a tight unit. We don't just have each other's backs—we are each other's backs. We've cried while putting down three pets, and hope we can be strong enough for each other when it really matters, when we have to go through something much harder. All we can do is keep talking, keep pace with the other's changing, and, if all else fails, as I once wrote to Kim in the last line of a poem: "We can run like hell together."

KATE BARKER is an award-winning writer and editor who has been published in many Canadian consumer magazines, including *Explore*, *Canadian Geographic Travel*, *Cottage Life*, and others. She is also an instructor at Ryerson University's School of Journalism. She lives in Toronto with her wife, potter Kim Henderson.

About a Butch

MAYA SAIBIL

AN OLD COWBOY WALKS into a bar and orders a whisky. A young woman sits down next to him. She turns to the cowboy and asks, "Are you a real cowboy?"

"Well, I've spent my whole life on the ranch, herding horses, mending fences, and branding cattle, so I guess I am," he replies.

"Well, I'm a lesbian," she says. "I spend my whole day thinking about women. As soon as I get up in the morning, I think about women. When I shower, I think about women. As I watch TV, or even eat, I think about women. Everything seems to make me think about women."

The two drink in silence. A short time later, a man sits down on the other side of the cowboy and asks, "Are you a real cowboy?"

"I always thought I was," he replies, "but I just found out that I'm a lesbian."

I remember hearing this joke and thinking it was hilarious, I suppose because I could relate to it. In my early gay days, I thought about women and my lesbian identity constantly. I had *lesbian* on my mind from the moment I woke up to the moment I went to bed (and girl-on-girl dreams throughout the night). I defined myself by my sexual orientation and wanted everyone to know it. I had a rite-of-passage, super-short lesbian haircut, watched *The L Word* religiously, listened to the Indigo Girls, played on a (mostly) lesbian hockey team, went to lesbian nightclubs (my first time out, I ran into my high school math teacher), and told lesbian jokes (see above).

Why was being gay so important to me? Because for one of the first times in my life, I found a "group" where I could be myself. I guess I had always thought of myself as different — like my idea of being a girl was not the same as what my peers thought. Hanging out with other gay women gave me that feeling of fitting in that I needed so badly. I was finally comfortable with myself.

A big part of my happiness was also due to the fact that I had started dating my childhood friend Vanessa, who remains my partner to this day. Vanessa was eighteen when we started dating, and I was seventeen. Coming out to family and friends was hard at times but made easier by the fact that I was doing it alongside my soul mate. When Vanessa told her mom she was gay, her mom reacted with sadness. She assumed this meant that Vanessa wouldn't have children, and she had hoped that her daughter would experience the joys of parenthood. Vanessa, however, had wanted to be pregnant and have children ever since she was a kid, and being gay wasn't going to stop her.

I, too, had always envisioned myself with kids but not pregnant. I actually specifically did not want to be pregnant, although I probably couldn't have articulated why at the time. Looking back, I think that as part of my need to be an obvious member of the gay community, I exaggerated the telltale signs of being a lesbian. To me, this meant adopting a stereotypical, and therefore easily identifiable, lesbian persona: a *butch* persona. With this persona came rules, rules that I was happy to follow: get a short haircut, develop "masculine" mannerisms, shop in the men's department, play a "manly" sport, don't carry a purse, don't wear makeup, don't be "overly emotional" in public, and certainly do *not* get pregnant or, worse—breastfeed. I had an image to uphold of being a tough, hockey-playing dyke, and I wasn't prepared to undermine it. So Vanessa and I didn't even need to discuss who would carry when we decided we were ready to have a baby.

When we were in our early twenties, we joined the Women's Hockey Club of Toronto, a recreational league for gay and gay-positive women ages sixteen to sixty-five. Playing in this league was the first time Vanessa and I met and became friends with lesbian moms. We always knew it was possible for lesbian couples to be parents and that families with same-sex parents existed, but getting to know happy, functioning families with two moms solidified the idea for us that having kids was not only theoretical but possible. We asked our gay mom friends tons of questions, and when we were in our mid-twenties, we started planning for a little one of our own.

The planning was all about getting sperm. I was partial to going with an anonymous donor, mostly because I was afraid a known donor might agree to a "give and go" scenario but then change his mind and want parental rights once the child was born. (In Canada, a biological father cannot legally sign away his parental rights until after the child is born.) But the idea of going with an unknown donor also scared the shit out of us. Apart from the diseases and medical conditions that sperm banks screen for, a lot of other information you get in a sperm donor's profile is self-reported and unverified, so who knows if it can be trusted? We decided to explore the known-donor route. Many interesting and awkwardly hilarious conversations later, we had asked ten men for sperm. But for reasons ranging from "I don't have kids of my own yet so I don't know how I'll feel when the kid is born" to "I've had a vasectomy," we didn't find our guy. So an anonymous donor it was, and I have to admit, I was a little relieved. Perhaps I felt threatened by the fact that a known donor would, by default, have more parental rights than me to my child if he chose to pursue them.

I made it my mission to select the sperm. Being the parent who would not be biologically related to our child, I enjoyed how choosing a donor from a sperm bank would make me a more active member in the baby-making process (Vanessa was happy because this meant she didn't have to sift through endless donor catalogues). I liked the feeling that I was in control of the sperm and getting Vanessa pregnant. Maybe this is how male partners feel? All I knew was that it felt good. It felt very butch. And it's what Ellen does in *If These Walls Could Talk 2*.

We asked our doctor friend David for advice on choosing sperm. His only suggestion was that we choose someone tall, since Vanessa and I are both on the short side, and tall people tend to have an easier time in life. We agreed that this made sense. Only months later did we realize that David's comment about both of us being short was funny because my height would obviously have no bearing on the height of our child. But we enjoyed the fact that his comment seemed to make perfect sense at the time because it assumed that Vanessa and I were making the baby together, which we were—we just weren't both contributing from a genetic perspective.

After narrowing our search to about five donors, we looked for what we called "Phelps sperm," after Olympic swimmer Michael Phelps. Since we weren't marrying the guy and there were plenty of donors who met our simple criteria, we decided to do our bank account a favour and make the final decision based on which sperm would reach the finish line first. We were on a tight budget and it would cost us sixteen hundred dollars for every cycle we inseminated. With the image of sperm reaching an egg at lightning speed in my mind, I called a sperm bank and asked, "Can you give me the motility counts for the following sperm donors?" Thinking about it now, I probably shouldn't have made that call from my open-concept cubicle at work.

We ordered the stuff, our doctor pinpointed Vanessa's ovulation, and it was finally time to make a baby. We arrived at our fertility clinic on a Friday morning for what our doctor referred to as Sperm Day. The guys in the white coats thawed and "washed" our sperm to prepare it for insemination. After waiting for what seemed like hours for our names to be called, we were ushered into a little room where the magic would happen. There was an "insemination table" and a funny, window-sized door at eye level.

What happened next was a bit rushed, not very romantic, but also kind of fun. Our doctor entered the room, opened the funny little door, reached through, and was handed a vial of sperm from one of the guys in white coats. I remember looking at the sperm and feeling happy, even strangely proud of myself. Yup, I chose that sperm. I rocked. The doctor then showed me a form with the donor number and sperm count to confirm that it was indeed donor No. 83162 as we had ordered. When I asked our doctor if I could inject the sperm into Vanessa, she was happy to let me do it but didn't seem to understand why I would want to. But I wanted to feel like *I* was getting Vanessa pregnant. As the doctor left the room, she instructed Vanessa to stay lying down and relax for five to ten minutes. "I'll leave you two now for your romance time," she said, switching on the radio as she walked out. The song playing was "Celebration" by Kool & the Gang. Vanessa and I waited until the door closed behind her before we burst out laughing.

We went back to the clinic the following morning to inseminate again, even though we were convinced that the pregnancy had already taken (most clinics recommend inseminating the day of ovulation as well as the day after to maximize your chances). After all, the second dose of sperm was paid for and waiting for us, and what kind of baby-wanting lesbians let perfectly good sperm go to waste? There is no way of knowing if it was the first or second squirt that took, but we do know that it worked. Two weeks later, we found out we were pregnant, and apart from Vanessa's mild morning queasiness, it felt awesome.

As the due date approached, we became more and more excited to meet our son or daughter. We registered for weekly email updates from the website BabyCenter about the development of our unborn child (I could have never expected that comparing the size of my baby to various types of fruit would be so interesting). We did a pregnancy photo shoot. We bought tiny onesies with cute phrases like "Got Milk?" written on them. We stocked up on newborn diapers. We even took prenatal classes. I admit that I felt a bit uncomfortable being the only gay couple in one of our classes, but the feeling passed quickly. Other than that, I hardly ever stopped to think about the fact that we were two women having a baby.

On July 24, 2009, we got to meet our perfect baby boy. Seeing my son, Cameron, being born was the happiest, most anticipated, most emotional moment of my life. But within minutes, he began having difficulty breathing and that happiness turned to fear. The pediatrician came urgently and started pumping air into Cameron's lungs. I stood beside Cameron, talking to him, trying to comfort him. For some reason, this annoyed the pediatrician because before telling us what the hell was going on, he demanded to know: "Who's the mother here?"

I had been a parent for fewer than five minutes and had already experienced sheer happiness, paralyzing fear, and homophobia. I froze and said nothing. Vanessa, who was lying on the delivery bed with copious amounts of blood oozing out of her, answered, "We both are." Not liking her answer, the pediatrician then explained the situation without making eye contact with either of us. Within a few minutes, Cameron was breathing fine, Vanessa's bleeding was under control, and the asshole doctor was out of our lives.

In the months that followed, our experience as new parents was pretty typical. We were completely clueless (despite having read the *What to Expect* books), permanently exhausted, didn't have sex anymore, talked about our son's poo at the dinner table, and, most importantly, were happy.

My sexual orientation was not something I really thought about anymore, but the fact that we were two moms came in handy when we decided we wanted a second child. Cameron was seven months old, Vanessa was about to defend her PhD dissertation, and I was getting ready to go back to work after my parental leave. The plan was to move to England in a few months for Vanessa to do a post-doctoral fellowship at Oxford University, and we figured out that if we got pregnant within the next couple of months, I would qualify for parental leave from Canada—which would certainly help us afford living in England.

Although we wanted another baby, the timing wasn't right for Vanessa to get pregnant again, as she was about to start a new job. I, on the other hand, would be unemployed in a foreign country, probably without the right to work. I didn't especially want to be pregnant, but I realized that I wasn't as opposed to it as I had been in the past. The idea of maintaining the butch lesbian image that once meant so much to me just didn't seem as important anymore—or maybe it was the twenty-five thousand dollar maternity leave carrot dangling before me? Whatever the reason, it was on a drive from Montreal to Toronto, while eating Timbits and sharing an extra-large double-double with Vanessa, that I decided to give the whole pregnancy thing a shot. This was my logic: If I didn't like it, at least it would be over in forty weeks and I'd have a baby at the end of it. And if I did like it, I'd be glad I did it. There was very little to lose and a lot to gain.

This time, getting pregnant was even less romantic. We were spending the week in Montreal with our families for Passover when an at-home ovulation monitoring kit indicated my body was ready for action. We had nothing planned for the next day that I couldn't get out of, so I took the overnight coach to Toronto while Vanessa stayed in Montreal with baby Cameron. When our doctor saw that I had come for the insemination, she laughed and called it the "Passover rush."

I knew the drill from last time. I asked the guys in the lab coats to thaw the sperm (from the same unknown donor as last time) and waited for my turn. When I went into the baby-making room, I called Vanessa on my cell phone. The doctor came in and I put Vanessa on speakerphone so that she could "be there" for the insemination (if we had had iPhones, we could have had insemination FaceTime). As I walked out once it was over, I wished our doctor a Happy Passover and made my way back to the bus station. I was in Toronto for no more than a few hours but had managed to get myself knocked up.

Even though this was my first time being pregnant, I felt like I had done it before because I had been so involved with Vanessa's pregnancy. And although I felt physically and emotionally uncomfortable at times, I loved feeling the baby's movements inside of me and I liked looking at my growing belly in the mirror—largely because I was amazed that there was a baby growing inside of me. Before I knew it, I was eight months along and we had moved to England. Six weeks later, Oliver, Cameron's brother from another mother, was born.

I would be lying if I said that I loved being pregnant, but I do love that I did it. I even breastfed Oliver—something I could never have pictured myself doing in my earlier super-butch phase. Eventually, even breastfeeding felt so natural that I hardly ever thought twice before whipping out my boobs in public. Being pregnant and breastfeeding helped me move away from the butch persona I thought I needed to adopt in order to be my true self, and ultimately helped me embrace my womanhood. When I first came out and started hanging out with other lesbians and integrating myself into the gay community, I thought I was being totally myself. And maybe I was. But the reality is, I have never felt more comfortable with myself as I do now that I have children. My kids are, pretty much, my life. Yes, I'm also a partner and a writer and a daughter and a hundred other things. But if someone ever sits down next to me at a bar and asks, "Are you a real lesbian?," my answer will be, "I always thought I was, but I have since discovered that I'm a mom."

MAYA SAIBIL is an advertising copywriter at TAXI, in Montreal, and a former magazine journalist. She is also a loving partner, a loyal friend, an okay hockey player, a good daughter, a proud sister, and a pretty good cook. But above all, she's a devoted mother.

A Matter of Perspective

BRUCE GILLESPIE

WHEN I WAS FOURTEEN and about to begin high school, my family moved from a metastasizing suburb of Toronto to a small northern Ontario paper mill town. Check that—we actually took up residence on an eighty-acre parcel of bush outside of town, down a rutted dirt road with the unlikely name of Pleasant Valley. It was a nice enough place to spend the holidays, as we'd done for a number of years, building tree houses and exploring old logging trails. Living there was another matter. Although I was decidedly not as worldly as I considered myself at the time, I'd spent years sneering at the local kids and their out-of-style haircuts, slightly twangy dialect, and inexplicable penchant for hockey and something called slo-pitch.

What confused me most about the town, though, was how

everyone seemed to know one another; indeed, they all seemed to be related. On one of my first days of school, a young woman with a short, frizzy perm accosted me in the hall outside of the auto shop, told me we shared a surname, and demanded to know how we were related. She seemed shocked when I informed her—in my haughtiest tone, I'm sorry to say—that there was no possible way we were family as I wasn't biologically related to anyone in the area. And with that, I stormed off, more convinced than ever that I'd landed in an enclave of inbred hicks.

I'm not sure who was more surprised: her, who had genuinely never come across anyone with the same uncommon surname that she wasn't related to, or me, at her assumption that we *must* have been cousins of some declension. But my experience of family was different from a lot of other kids I knew. In the city, we were surrounded by Italian and Portuguese kids whose extended families all seemed to live within a ten-block radius, who hung out with their cousins, and who visited their grandparents on a regular basis. My extended family had never resembled theirs. As a kid, I moved around a lot. Each time my father got a promotion, we moved farther and farther away. It wasn't intentional; it just worked out that way. So, while both sets of my grandparents and the rest of my extended family lived within an hour's drive of one another in the Ottawa Valley, we moved farther away, slowly shifting out of their orbit. We'd visit them once or twice a year, but we weren't especially close, not like the families in my new home.

It was the sort of town where most people's lives stretched out ahead of them in fairly predictable ways. You'd graduate from high school, maybe attend university in nearby Sudbury or North Bay, marry someone you'd grown up with, and, if you were lucky, land a job at the mill and return home. You'd have kids who would grow up to treat their cousins as pseudo siblings and have dinner with their grandparents down the street once or twice a week.

Although I would not have admitted it back then, I was a little jealous of the certainty most of my classmates seemed to have about the direction of their lives, even if I disagreed with their compass bearings. One of the hardest parts about growing up gay in such a small, rural community was that there was no one else like me around. At a time when all of my friends were starting to try their adult lives on for size by dating, having sex, and meeting potential life mates, I was alone. Even though I had a small circle of close friends and a larger network of acquaintances, cultivated mostly through the drama club and school newspaper, what I remember most about high school was feeling lonely, a gnawing in the pit of my stomach that ran in the background to my otherwise happy life, a constant reminder that I'd never be happy because I would never find someone who would love me. As my friends would share their stories about hooking up or dating woes, I'd listen patiently and wonder, Why not me? My high school years felt like purgatory, in which I became a bystander to everyone else's lives, which I came to accept as suitable training for the rest of my life.

At the time, I simply couldn't imagine what lay ahead of me—and not for any lack of actual imagination on my part. I knew it would involve hopping the first Greyhound bus out of town as soon as I graduated, but otherwise I was clueless. Although I knew a couple of queer people—a childhood friend of my mother's and a former co-worker from her job in the city—I had no clear sense of how they lived or what their lives were like. And, as far as I could tell, there were no queer people in town. If there were, they must have kept a low profile, probably a wise move in a town with more independent, unaffiliated churches than stoplights.

Eventually, I turned to books for some idea of what a gay life could be. (It's the story of my life: if I want to understand something, I need to read about it.) It being the early 1990s, my options were limited. But by some struck of luck, the local public library carried a copy of American writer Paul Monette's *Borrowed Time: An AIDS Memoir*, first published in 1990. The book is a beautifully written but harrowing account of the early years of the plague and the death of Monette's lover, Roger. In stark, heartbreaking detail, Monette relates how gay men, ignored by most of the medical system and often ostracized by frightened family and friends, banded together to support one another. It was a grim window into gay life for a closeted teen like myself, but at least it was something. It was proof that gay men who came out of the closet had lives and friends and could even find love, if at a high and often mortal cost. For me, it was a scant sliver of hope because at the time, although I secretly hoped that I might one day find a man to settle down with, I was more or less resigned to leading a quiet, solitary life. But one thing was for sure—if nothing else, I would live in a city, where I might be able to meet other gay people or, at the very least, blend into the crowds and carve out the kind of anonymous life that small towns do not afford.

That's pretty much how it happened too. After my five

required years of high school, I left home to study in Ottawa and, later, Toronto. One of my first goals was simply to meet people my age like me. I wanted the assurance that I'd found a place where queer people could live their lives openly, but I was also looking for love. And sex. Or some combination of the two. Like many gay men of my generation, I experienced a delayed adolescence, spending my early twenties learning the lessons about dating that my straight friends had learned as teenagers—figuring out how relationships worked, what I wanted from one, and how difficult it was to find a good match. Before moving to the city, I had assumed that I would have a lot in common with every gay man I met, but I soon found out that, regardless of sexual orientation, people are just people. Some you get along with, some you don't; some you want to date, many you do not. In short, I started to realize that simply living in a big city and being out did not feel as fulfilling as I thought it would. But I took comfort in the fact that I lived in a place where I could live my life honestly. Even if I wasn't happy, at least I was living life on my own terms and far away from my small town existence, which I felt sure could never hold any kind of satisfying future for me.

Until I met Greg, that is. The first time we met was while I was attending university in Ottawa and took a Thanksgiving road trip to my best friend's hometown of Simcoe, a town of about fifteen thousand people near the Lake Erie shore. While there, I met Greg, an old high school chum of my best friend. He was unlike most of the guys I'd dated, who were overconfident egoists more interested in acquiring a fan than a partner. Greg was none of those things: he was kind and charming in an old-fashioned, gentlemanly kind of way. And he had a smile that could light up a room, something I'd read about in novels but assumed was merely a turn of phrase. We hit it off instantly, but as he had just started dating someone and I lived six hours away, nothing came of it except for a love letter. I can't remember how it happened, but somehow we ended up talking about love letters and he said he had never received one, which I thought was a shame. So, when I returned home, I wrote him one—a mostly fictional one, of course, because I hardly knew him, and one that played to all of the tropes of love letters (scented stationery, an upside-down stamp). He didn't write back, so I wasn't even sure he had received it and thought no more of it.

We met again five or six years later when I was living and working in Toronto and my best friend, who had moved home to Simcoe by this point, invited me to join her and Greg and a few friends on their regular Saturday-night trip to what passed as the local gay bar. It was an offer I couldn't resist, not only because I wanted to catch up with Greg, who I knew was single at this point, but also to see what a country gay bar was like. With visions of straw bales and line dancing, I figured it would make a great story to tell my friends back in the city over martinis at a real bar, if nothing else.

What I had imagined was not far from the truth. In the first place, the bar wasn't really a bar at all, rather a derelict agricultural hall on the outskirts of town that an older lesbian couple rented during the spring and fall for invitation-only dances; if you didn't know someone on the membership list who could vouch for you, you weren't admitted. Unlike most gay bars I had visited in larger cities, this one was an almost equal mix of men and women and young and old. There were few designer labels in the crowd: light-wash blue jeans, plaid shirts, and cowboy boots were the order of the day.

As with most nights at The Robin's Nest, as the hall was known on dance nights, things got under way with country waltzes that the older couples danced to. As the night wore on and the place filled up, the DJ—one of the fifty-something lesbians who rented the hall—switched to mostly Top 40 dance music with a line dancing number thrown in every three or four songs, which packed the floor. By midnight, there must have been a hundred and fifty or two hundred people there, and apart from the queer vibe, it resembled nothing so much as the country wedding receptions I had attended growing up. Greg seemed to know most of the people there, easily moving from one conversation to the next, as is his way. At the beginning of the evening, I felt a bit jealous, but toward the end of the evening, he was spending more time with me. We went home together that night and have been together ever since.

While neither of us had been looking for a long-term relationship, it just happened that way because, as hopelessly romantic as it sounds, we had a hard time being apart. I'd visit him in Simcoe on the weekends, and every Sunday he'd balk at dropping me off at the train station and drive me back into the city instead, where he'd spend the night and then head home early in the morning to work at the restaurant he owned at the time. I was a freelance journalist back then, so I started taking long weekends in Simcoe, as it was easy enough for me to work from Greg's apartment. Those long weekends stretched into weeks, and eventually I found myself contemplating something unimaginable: moving to Simcoe in order to be with him.

Although it sounded crazy, it didn't feel crazy; it felt like the only way to soothe the ache I felt on the days when I didn't see him and distracted me from work. None of my friends or family seemed to think it was crazy either. Us together, being together, just seemed right. Moving an hour and a half outside of the city, especially with as a flexible job as I had, just made sense. So, within a matter of months, I went from the sort of anonymous life in the city, surrounded by a close network of friends, that I'd always dreamed of as a teenager to the small town life I had once forsworn.

In short order, I realized that where you live is less important than who you live with, and that's thanks to Greg. Through his example, he showed me that it's possible to live a happy, fulfilling life as an openly gay man in a rural community. Indeed, we've created a good life for ourselves. We have two dogs and live in a lovely red-brick century home right downtown, where we're on excellent terms with our neighbours, none of whom blinked at a couple of gay guys moving into the neighbourhood (and some of whom even dropped off a thoughtful sympathy card upon reading about another local gay man who had died, thinking it was me. It's the thought that counts, I told myself). Greg is well known and well liked in this community, so everywhere we go, he's stopped by someone who wants to catch up. While I sometimes miss the anonymity of living in a bigger city, and being able to grocery shop or eat in a restaurant without inter-ruption, I've come to appreciate this kind of connection—that people here aren't so wrapped up in their work or their own lives that they want to take ten or twenty minutes wherever they happen to meet you to chat. Although the idea of being so known, so public, bothered me as a teenager, when I was fearful that being known meant being revealed for who I really was, now that I'm out of the closet, I don't really have any secrets and so don't mind a bit of notoriety in being one of the handful of openly queer folks in the area.

Fortunately, being a gay couple doesn't seem to matter to most people we've met here. We don't even get awkward glances from the guys who come to clean the furnace or reshingle the roof. We even have our regular haunts, including a bakery on the highway out of town, which caters mostly to the after-church crowd on Sundays and farmers, where the waitresses know our orders and look to me when Greg debates between a salad or fries and ask in a good-natured way if he's allowed to go greasy, as though I have any say in the matter.

One of the foundations of the life we have here is the family we've created for ourselves, in which I include the folks we're related to as well as the many friends who over the years have become much more than the term suggests. We have a good relationship with Greg's parents, both of whom live just blocks away, and see them regularly for dinner and holidays. We have made many good friends who have included us in their own families as we have done for them. Some are straight; some are queer. Some are older, some are younger. Some live nearby, while others live hours away. Some are childless, like us, while others have kids, whom we delight in seeing and even babysitting from time to time.

Our lives aren't perfect. We bicker about all sorts of things, like whose turn it is to cut the grass (his) or take out the garbage (mine), and we're both workaholics who have trouble taking time off. But when it comes to the issues that really matter, we work well together. We've supported each other through major career changes, sudden and unexpected deaths in our families, and all of the other ups and downs that couples encounter over fourteen years. It is, hands down, a far happier ending than I ever had cause to expect for myself as a teenager. And while I cringe to think of how my younger self might judge the choices I've made, particularly in terms of where I chose to live, I think he'd also be happy, maybe even surprised and relieved, that I've found someone to love and who loves me back. Like that teenager, I still have trouble figuring out what lies ahead, but I'm okay with that, knowing that whatever comes my way, I'll have someone to share it with and who will stand beside me.

BRUCE GILLESPIE is an assistant professor in the digital media and journalism program at Wilfrid Laurier University's Brantford campus. He is the co-editor of *Somebody's Child: Stories About Adoption* and *Nobody's Father: Life Without Kids*, both published by TouchWood Editions. He is also the editor-in-chief of J-Source.ca | The Canadian Journalism Project. He lives in Simcoe, Ontario, near the Lake Erie shore.

Created by Choice

DALE LEE KWONG

I DON'T BELIEVE THE old adage that says you can pick your friends but not your family. When you're adopted, as I was, you know it isn't true. But it's not just birth parents and adoptive parents who make these decisions—every person can design, alter, and trim the fabric that becomes their family through the choices they make. Family is much more than a blood connection; family is the people we choose to surround ourselves with for support. Sometimes they're blood relatives, but family can just as easily include co-workers, business associates, good friends, neighbours, or even a community of people who share a hobby, religion, ethnicity, or point of view.

Chinese by birth, I was blessed to be adopted and raised in a Chinese Canadian home. Pride in my ethnicity gave me a solid foundation to explore and build my identity. Family is highly regarded in Chinese social structure, and my parents nurtured this value. Tragically, my first adoptive mother died of kidney failure before I was seven, but my father later remarried, and his new wife insisted on legally adopting me too. My father was a steady presence in my life, and his strength of character guides me and inspires me to this day. His legacy is a powerful example of accomplishment through hard work and generosity in business, family, philanthropy, and community service.

My grandfather came to Canada from China in 1886. He settled in Vernon, British Columbia, with two wives. My father was one of fifteen children raised by the two mothers. Although First Wife and her children received some special treatment, the two mothers were said to be like sisters, and family unity and goals trumped those of individuals. It was at home that my father first learned that family was more than bloodlines. The Chinese community in Vernon was tight knit and supportive of one another; they likely bonded over the hardships created by the Chinese Exclusion Act, which restricted the immigration of Chinese people to Canada and imposed a head tax.

My father's definition of family included anyone whose ideals reflected his own, regardless of race, religion, or social standing. Perhaps because he was a single parent for a time, my father embraced the notion that it takes a village to raise a child. It was therefore not unusual for me to call his clients or business associates and their wives Uncle and Auntie. This included, but was not limited to, his lawyer and accountant. When my father remarried and honeymooned in Europe for the summer, it was Uncle Don and Auntie Margie—my father's doctor and his wife—who cared for my sister and me at their Windermere cabin. My friends wondered how I could have so many Caucasian relatives, but I never thought to explain something I thought every family did, adopting those who embraced us as family.

Of course, our family also included my father's actual relatives. With my father coming from such a large nuclear family, it's no surprise that my extended family is huge. What shocks most people, though, is the fact that I know most of my relatives, even two generations above and below my own. In large part it's because my father's generation started organizing family reunions when I was a teenager, and it's a tradition that has continued ever since. Split mostly between Alberta and British Columbia, there were more than eighty family members at KFR 2012 in Vancouver. Plans are already afoot for KFR 2014 in Calgary.

In Chinese culture, it is tradition for families to gather to open and close the two-week New Year's celebration with a dinner. The ten-course banquet meal is served slowly and can take two to three hours. In Calgary, we generally do one dinner with our nuclear family and one with our extended. At our most recent celebration, one cousin was housebound due to illness. During one of the lulls between courses, we learned she had bought a new cell phone and decided to tease her by anonymously texting photos of the meal she was missing. When she asked who we were, we replied mysteriously, with comments like, "I'm the one eating your dumplings." We even forwarded photos from Calgary to cousins in Vancouver and asked them to text her from their long-distance numbers. At the end of the evening, we culprits took a photo of ourselves and sent it to our hapless target. I love my extended family: we have a lot of fun, and I've always counted my cousins and second cousins among my closest friends. Now that my generation is raising children, we aspire to pass the same strong family values on to the next generation.

It hasn't all been rainbows and butterflies, though. I've had a few bumps in the road with my adoptive family regarding my sexual orientation. I suspect it would have been easier if I'd had the courage to come out to my father, but I was afraid to jeopardize our relationship and didn't understand the depth of his unconditional love until he was gone. While waiting in the emergency examination room during some cardiac distress, my father made a point of telling me about his friend's gay son. He giggled and said the two of them went to Stampeder football games together. We'd never had a conversation like that before. The only time I can recall something like it, he joked about seeing former member of parliament Svend Robinson in our hotel lobby the summer before. I wasn't sure which part of the story amused him: that someone we knew was homosexual, that a gay man attended a sporting event, or that his friend had accepted his son's sexual orientation. My father had seen a lot of changes in attitudes toward gays and lesbians in his eighty years; I couldn't determine the point he was making. After he was discharged, I drove him home. He tousled my hair, told me I was a good kid, and we hugged goodbye.

That was the last time I saw my father; he suffered a massive coronary attack days later. It was then that I understood the significance of our conversation and the opportunity he was trying to give me. He had met my then girlfriend and knew we were planning to buy a house together, but I'd lied and explained it as a business investment. When he asked what would happen if either of us got married, presumably to a man, I punched him in the arm and said it would never happen. I've since concluded that he understood and accepted my sexual orientation.

A month later, I came out to my second adoptive mother. It was the night before my father's will was being read. I wasn't sure how she would feel about having a lesbian daughter, so I decided full disclosure was the best course of action. Somehow, I imagined her finding out on her own, accusing me of being dishonest, and then disowning me, so it was a pre-emptive strike. After delivering my news, I'm not sure who was shaking more. My mother didn't believe me at first, but when she realized I wasn't joking, she assured me she had no intention of disowning me. She wondered why I might think that, and I believe she was even a bit offended at the suggestion. Still, it didn't stop her from leaving the room whenever my then partner walked in, and it took years to gain her acceptance.

It was the embrace of the rest of our family that helped my mother come to terms with my sexual orientation. That process began within a month of my coming out to my mother. After a family dinner she hosted, I methodically called family members to the basement to share the news I was gay and in a relationship with the person they knew as my friend. I'd asked permission to do this from my mother; she simply resigned herself to the fact that she couldn't stop me. It went relatively well: the seniors said life was short and who were they to judge? My cousins said they'd known for years. Surprisingly, it was the middle-aged relatives who offered explanations and excuses for my sexual orientation. Perhaps it was a phase? Perhaps I hadn't met the right man? It was even suggested I might consider dating a non-Asian. I stifled a laugh, realizing that my partner was not only of the wrong gender, but also not of the expected race. Considering it was the early 1990s, and Ellen DeGeneres hadn't even come out yet, it's remarkable how my traditional, Chinese family responded. Many were even happy for me.

Still, what real family doesn't have a bit of drama? Mine involved an incident with my uncle's wife. Throughout the years, Auntie X hosted dinners with both sides of the family, hers and ours. After my uncle passed away, she continued the tradition and co-hosted with her sisters. After I came out to the family, I insisted my then partner be included in family invitations and everyone complied. However, because of our jobs, we were often unable to attend. So, we were happy to receive an invitation one year to a Chinese banquet-style dinner that both of us could accept.

The last to arrive, we discovered there was a formal seating plan for dinner. Normally, couples sat together, so I was surprised to be told that my partner and I would sit at separate tables. The aunties said they wanted to mix things up by splitting some of the couples. It seemed like a reasonable enough explanation, so we sat in our designated seats and I didn't question the arrangement.

As I got settled and looked around, I realized that of the fifteen or so couples there, only two were separated—me and my partner and a gay man and his partner on my aunt's side of the family. All of the heterosexual couples sat with their significant others, not just at the same table but side by side. I wondered if it was an oversight, but the more I thought about it, the more I realized it was by design. I hadn't experienced such blatant discrimination since being teased about my ethnicity in elementary school. I was shocked to be treated this way by family.

Unsure of how to respond, I conferred with my partner. While we agreed the slight was deliberate, she wasn't convinced it was malicious. I then compared notes with the other segregated couple. They, too, felt excluded and unwelcome; I wasn't imagining things or being hypersensitive. The four of us agreed the seating arrangement was homophobic, but no one wanted to make a fuss. The aunties ranged in age from mid-seventies to late-eighties, and none of us wanted to confront or embarrass them. Dinner was already being served, and there was no way to slip out of the restaurant without making a scene.

Despite my humiliation, I was convinced to stay. My anger has not dissipated over the years, but my submissive response has. If something like this were to happen again, I would make a scene. Age and ignorance are no longer acceptable excuses and probably never were. Never again did I accept a dinner invitation from this aunt and her sisters; the circumstances were unforgivable and this hurt has not healed. Still, family is what you make it, and it's all about choices, isn't it? While I have not forgotten this incident, I continue to build a relationship with my aunt. My sister, mother, and I even took a vacation with Auntie X and her daughter. It's not my place to educate my auntie and her sisters, but I can honour our long history without compromising myself.

I had already compromised myself for years, reaching my

early thirties before realizing I was a lesbian. I'd fallen in love with girlfriends throughout my life, but this time I dared do something about it, and the risk paid off: I discovered that a close friend from church was in love with me too. It was pretty confusing for both of us; after all, we'd met at a bible study and considered ourselves evangelical Christians. In the beginning, neither of us believed we were lesbians—we believed we had fallen in love with the spirit of another person and that spirit just happened to reside in another female body. It was a simplistic explanation that made the situation more palatable as we wrestled our faith with our sexuality. Instinctively, I distanced myself from church friends who I later learned could not accept my sexual orientation. They believed I had a choice in the matter, when I did not. The only choice I had was whether to be honest with myself or not.

For ten years my partner and I created our version of domestic bliss. Neither of us had been married or involved in long-term romantic relationships with men, so we had no rules or gender expectations in the relationship; we knew our strengths and played to them. If I cooked, she cleaned and vice versa. I designed and watered the garden; she planted and weeded it. We celebrated each other's cultural heritage: I knew the secret to good borsch was adding canned pork and beans at the table and she made a mean stir-fry. A trained classical musician, she practised musical scales that I would dance to, and I introduced her to Melissa Etheridge. We raised three dogs that added fullness to our family life.

We helped each other through the coming-out process to our friends, family, and co-workers. We bought a home in the burbs and created a haven from the worries of the world. We hosted mah-jong, sushi, and potluck parties. We worshipped together and attended weddings and family reunions together. In many ways, it was the most hetero-normative time of my life. However, the learning curve was steep and often challenging, as we had never problem-solved through a relationship before. Fundamental in some of my religious beliefs was the idea that thinking about something was just as sinful as actually committing a transgression. While attending a writing conference, I found myself crushing on another woman and so I returned home to abruptly break up with my partner even though I had committed no wrong. It's crazy when I look back on it, but it made sense to me at the time. Once I'd made the decision, there was no changing my mind. Somewhere along the way, I had grown away from my partner and fallen out of love.

Since then, I have spent more years out of relationships than in them. Fortunately, I have a lot of friends in my life that I consider family. The closest is my best friend, whom I've known since kindergarten. I'd love to say we've been friends all those years between then and now, but the only reason I know about our kindergarten connection is because our parents told us. We reconnected at a church retreat after graduating from university, and we haven't looked back since.

Over the course of thirty years we've shared a lot of laughs at home and abroad. She was the first person I came out to. The stakes were high, but I needed to know. We were attending an evangelical Baptist church at the time, and I was sure she would reject me. I stalled with so many introductory words and tears that she was relieved when I finally revealed my news.

She probably thought I was dying, and in some ways, I was. I was expecting to be asked to leave her apartment; instead, she offered me a hug. Wisely, she let love be her guide, unlike many other church friends.

Today, I have the privilege of being her son's godmother. He and his sister respectfully call me "Dale E-E" (*E-E* is a Chinese term that indicates I am an auntie related on the maternal side of the family). I always wondered when I should come out to the kids, but I never had to. They figured it out for themselves at a young age and were fine with my sexuality. I imagine they took their cues from their mother. Being hateful and discriminatory are learned behaviours; kids gravitate toward love and acceptance.

Since my godson is a gifted child, our relationship was somewhat adult-like from early on. Rather than me teaching him things, he is often the one teaching me. He delights in history and often surprises me with his knowledge of Calgary's history. Twice he has helped me take my mother to the Calgary Stampede. In her late eighties, she is slower and less steady on her feet than she used to be. Knowing she would have difficulty navigating the crowds, I forced her to agree to renting a wheelchair. It was a blow to her ego, but inviting my godson to come along softened it. He took such pride in pushing her around the grounds; he gave her a lot of attention, and in turn she treated us to the prime rib buffet.

Thanks to my experiences as a playwright in Calgary, I have been able to nurture my godson's love for live theatre. A few seasons ago, I facilitated his first shift as a volunteer usher for Lunchbox Theatre. I imagined my father beaming down at this legacy of volunteerism. Later that year, I proudly sat in the audience for his high school debut in *The Sound of Music* and this year watched him perform as Javert in *Les Misérables*.

Knowing I prefer gifts over gift cards, my best friend asked what they might give me for Christmas. On a visit to their house for dinner, I commented on their unique bowls and plates. When I discovered the kids had painted them, I said I'd love if they made me something. The kids thought it would be more fun to introduce me to the pottery store, so we agreed on a date. Unfortunately, my menopausal hormones were raging out of control that day. As the staff person explained the different glazes and techniques, my anxiety escalated and I started to cry. I left to compose myself but upon returning found myself bawling. I was a hot mess, and my godson was very concerned. On the other hand, his sister laughed and pointed at me, asking her mother, "What's wrong with Dale E-E?" She even mocked me a little, which helped diffuse the situation. Later in the day, the kids were already suggesting we make it an annual event. I said no, but by the next day, I saw the humour of the situation and agreed to try again. The kids are already looking forward to what they hope is an annual event—the pottery experience, not the hot mess auntie.

So, you see how blessed I am? Not only is my family of origin kind of crazy, so, too, is my extended adoptive family. I've barely scratched the surface of other best friends in the mix: a condo neighbour who comes over to watch reality TV, a co-worker who was a wonderful godmother to my border collie, and a former dog walker whose toddler son randomly screams my name at the top of his lungs when I visit their

Victoria home. When does someone cross the line from being friend to being family? It's hard to say, but I suspect it starts when they accept you unconditionally. Family is created by both circumstance and choice, and I am greatly blessed and have made wise decisions.

DALE LEE KWONG has been an ENG News Editor at Global Television for twenty-six years. She is also an award-winning playwright, published poet, and essayist with work in *Somebody's Child: Stories About Adoption*, *Modern Morsels*, *Canadian Literature*, and *splinterswerve*. She was a proud member of the Creation Ensemble for the inaugural production of Third Street Theatre, Calgary's queerest theatre company. She believes family is created by the choices we make.

Operation: Baby

JEFFREY RICKER

YOU HAVE TO BE pretty persuasive to get me to jerk off in a public bathroom. (That, or you have to be Chris Hemsworth.) Nevertheless, five years ago I found myself standing in the restroom at a doctor's office, one hand holding a plastic cup and the other hand —

Well, maybe I should back up and explain how this came to be.

I'll admit, I've never been partial to children, even when I was one of them. That expression, four going on forty? It may not have been coined for me, but it was used to describe me more than once. When my partner and I first got together, the topic of kids did come up. I think I said no before he even finished asking the question. "I'd consider adopting kids as long as they're old enough to dust" is an often-repeated line around our house and tells you two important things about Michael and me: one, we don't have the tidiest house in the world; and two, we don't have kids.

Much like marriage, child-rearing never seemed to be in the cards for me, and I was fine with that. More than fine, really; my brother and his wife have a great daughter, so I felt confident that our family's fairly above-average intelligence genes had been successfully passed on to the next generation. With that weight off my shoulders, I could concentrate on other things, like my career. On second thought, let's not talk about my career.

But then my friend—I'll call her Ann—said she had a favour to ask. There are few people outside my family that I've known (and liked) longer than her. We met in college, and though careers drew us into different orbits and different cities, we never lost touch. I knew she and her partner, Sara, wanted to have a family, so it shouldn't have come as a surprise to me when they said they were going to try artificial insemination.

Sara's sister probably had something to do with their decision. She was in the military, as was her husband (now ex-husband), and when they were both deployed, they needed someone to look after their one-year-old son, Eli. He was sent to stay with Ann and Sara, and for eighteen months the two of them became parents in all but name. Shortly before Eli's parents split up but after they returned from deployment and Eli went home, Ann and Sara decided they wanted this for themselves. Parenthood, that is. Not divorce.

They went through the process of selecting an anonymous Ivy League donor from a catalogue, got tested to see which of them stood the best chance of having a baby (Sara), and then they did it and crossed their fingers.

And nothing happened.

This, of course, was not necessarily unexpected. On average, it can take five to ten attempts before AI is successful. And while it's less expensive than in vitro fertilization, it's not exactly cheap, and Ivy League donors are an added expense. What if it took them even longer? They weren't getting any younger.

This is where the favour came in. Would I be willing to donate my—how should I put this—genetic information to them in hopes that they might successfully conceive?

In short, they wanted my junk.

I don't honestly remember if I hesitated before I said yes. I probably did. We tend to be environmentally minded, we Rickers—my parents live in the woods, and my brother runs a nature sanctuary. He and his wife decided to have only one kid because of the impact population growth has on the environment. Aren't there enough people on the planet, anyway?

But.

I could have said no, couldn't I? There was adoption, after all. But how much luck would two lesbians have if they tried to adopt a child? I live in St. Louis, a modestly liberal Midwestern city surrounded by a rabidly conservative state— Rush Limbaugh is from here, if that gives you any clue to how unhinged they are. Ann and Sara lived in similar circumstances in the South, and I could only guess how much trouble they would run into. Plus, adoption was a lengthy process and, like AI and IVF, it had a price tag. If they were lucky, they'd be parents before they qualified for senior citizen discounts.

After I said yes, there was paperwork to sign and contracts for me to surrender any and all claims to whatever child might be produced if we were successful. The forms arrived in the mail accompanied by a dollar bill: although I was going to do this as a volunteer, apparently a financial transaction was recommended to make the contract binding. I wonder what I did with that dollar; I probably bought a soda. Yes, my services can be had in exchange for a twenty-ounce Diet Coke. Cheap and easy.

But back to the men's room at the doctor's office. To make sure we weren't completely wasting our time (and that I wasn't shooting blanks), Ann and Sara arranged for me to take a fertility test at a nearby hospital. The results would be sent to them and their doctor, and then they'd decide whether it was worth going ahead. The nurse handed me a little plastic specimen cup and told me to head down the hall to the men's room. I guessed our conversation was all the foreplay I was going to get.

Fortunately, the men's room was a one-person-only facility, otherwise it might have been awkward. Still, the experience was surreal, if for no other reasons than these two: in this very institutional-looking bathroom—grey floor with a drain in it, white porcelain fixtures, a toilet with a seat but no lid; where was I supposed to sit?—there was a wicker basket containing an assortment of magazines intended to help those who needed a little, well, inspiration. Naturally, none of these were the sort that would inspire me, but we're talking about the Midwest here, so that's hardly a surprise.

The other surreal detail was the small latched door in the wall just next to the sink. This was where I was supposed to leave my sample once I'd finished. It made me think of the night deposit drop at a bank—or an especially clinical glory hole. I couldn't resist the urge to peer through, surprised that I could actually see the other side, disappointed that it looked like a nondescript lab with microscopes and test tubes, and relieved that no one saw me peeking through. What would I have done if I had seen someone, or if they'd reached through the opening thinking another sample was ready to be tested? Would I have let the door slap shut and left, told Ann and Sara I'd changed my mind, and sent the dollar back?

None of that happened, of course. A few weeks later I got a copy of the test results myself. Although I wasn't shooting blanks, I wasn't exactly shooting prime ammunition. I was diagnosed with a low sperm count and low motility—apparently, there weren't many swimmers and they were mostly treading water. I decided to stop riding my bike for a while, convinced it was pinching something that shouldn't be pinched. I also switched from boxer briefs to regular boxer shorts after reading an article I found online (the Internet: making it so much easier to obsess about everything) that stated a man's choice of underwear could make a temperature difference of a few degrees, which is apparently enough to overheat things down there.

A week or so later, the Styrofoam cooler arrived. Because Ann and Sara lived on the other side of the country, I'd have to FedEx the goods to them on a monthly basis, packed in dry ice and overnighted. The box was labelled "Horse Semen." According to Ann, thoroughbred breeders do this all the time, so that's what I told the FedEx clerk I was: a breeder.

Oh, the irony.

For four months we worked on Operation: Baby, as Ann and Sara called it. I'd get an email telling me to be on deck, as it were, followed by the signal to prep a delivery. Fill the little cup (well, not fill it—it wasn't that small), add this preservative to keep it viable for the trip, then pack it in the Styrofoam container along with the dry ice packs, box it all up, and take it to FedEx for overnight delivery. The handoff at FedEx was always the most nerve-wracking part: what if the clerk wanted to know more about what was in the box? If I told him "Exactly what it says on the outside," how bad a lie was that? What if he asked the name of my horse? Or what he looked like? (Conversely, I can only imagine how much more awkward it would have been if the post office allowed such deliveries: "Anything in the box liquid, fragile, or potentially hazardous?" How about all of the above?)

It's odd now to think of how much I was hoping this would be a success—mainly for Ann and Sara, who I was convinced would be phenomenal parents. If I'm honest though, I was hoping for success for myself as well. Why did I care, though? Maybe I didn't want to be a parent, but on some level, I *did* want to be a father, if only in an instinctual, biological imperative sort of way. I would have no formal role in the kid's life, if a kid did result from this science project. Maybe that made it easier: the accomplishment of fatherhood without the burden of parenthood.

I can count on one hand the number of times I've held a baby: My niece at her christening, in a small, un-air-conditioned church in the summer while sweat rolled down my spine. (She was a heavy baby by that point.) Once, at my friend Marie's October wedding, when one of her relatives or friends or someone plunked a baby in my lap and said, "I have to go to the bathroom, watch her." Once, when a co-worker brought her newborn to the office, and most recently at a friend's birthday party at a pub, when her brother handed over his son in order to eat a hamburger and maybe have some of his pint. For some reason, in each case the babies seemed perfectly at ease being held by me. (Also, I discovered that babies will put their fingers anywhere, including in someone's mouth or eyes or, in one instance, nose.) The nice thing about being handed someone else's baby is you are always free to hand him or her back.

In the end, the biological clock keeps ticking, priorities change, and Sara and Ann brought Operation: Baby to a close when it became clear we weren't having much luck in the process. Perhaps it's for the best that I didn't pass along my own (probably overstated) above-average intelligence since it comes with a helping of hereditary high cholesterol and heart disease, and a side of nearsightedness. I'm fond of saying that if I'd lived in prehistoric times, I'd have been eaten by the sabre-toothed tiger I never saw coming. Still, I suppose there are worse things to pass on to your kids, like stupidity and narrow-mindedness.

I consider myself lucky, though. The family I was born into still loves me, which I know is not always the case. I'd say we love one another without judgment, but if you've ever known anyone from New England, you'll know that would just be a big, fat lie. If we judge, though, we don't hold it against one another, and we may judge one another for what we say or do — or, most often, wear — but we don't judge one another for who we are. Some of my friends aren't so lucky. Sara still has issues with her father and his deep fundamentalist beliefs that keep him from fully accepting his daughter. Likewise with another friend whose family disowned him. In both cases, though, they've managed to gather around them a family that accepts and loves them as they are, no questions asked. Which, when I think about it, is why I said yes when Ann and Sara asked me to help them become parents. Because I knew they'd never stop loving a child if they had one.

And when things don't turn out the way we'd hoped, we make do. It's what queer people have always done: take a shitty situation and sift through it for something worth salvaging. I have no doubt that Sara and Ann would have been spectacular parents — certainly better than a lot of straight people I could point out. But you make do. Sometimes, maybe most of the time if you're gay, you have to work twice as hard to get half as much and consider yourself lucky. Maybe that will change sooner rather than later, I don't know. What I do know is that Ann now does volunteer work with underprivileged children in the court system, and she's damned good at helping pick up the pieces that careless people have damaged and cast aside.

Give us something broken and we'll fix it. We'll make it better than it was to begin with, even. We do it with houses, we do it with neighbourhoods, and when we need to, we do it with families.

JEFFREY RICKER's first novel, *Detours*, was published in 2011 by Bold Strokes Books. His second novel, the YA fantasy *The Unwanted*, will be published in 2014, and his short fiction and essays have appeared in more than a dozen anthologies. He is pursuing an MFA at the University of British Columbia and lives in St. Louis, Missouri. Keep up with his work at jeffrey-ricker.com.

The Gay Divorcée: How Marriage Equality Couldn't Save My Marriage

JEAN COPELAND

IT WAS ONE OF the most exciting days of my life, historic even, that day in 2006 when Connecticut's General Assembly passed civil union legislation. My insides grew all warm and squishy contemplating what this meant for my partner and me and lesbian and gay couples all over the state. To celebrate, in a dance club somewhere people would be triumphantly crowding the floor to a Donna Summer or Village People hit that gays had long ago adopted as one of our anthems. At last, the moment every long-suffering couple dreamed of had arrived: the straight world would have to acknowledge our love as authentic and as meaningful as theirs. My partner, Diana, and I would now have the chance to show that our love mattered in an official ceremony that would be recognized by our state government. Then, all that would be left was living happily ever after as woman and wife. Well, that's how I'd envisioned it anyway.

Diana and I had been together for fourteen years, and a civil union seemed like the last piece in the complex puzzle that had been our relationship. I envisioned how the scars from years of emotional struggle as we slowly inched our way out of the closet to friends and co-workers might begin to fade after the ceremony. Most importantly, it would be the acknowledgment from Diana I had been waiting for.

The big event was set in motion the night I was channel surfing and happened across a public access announcement for a Valentine's Day marathon of free marriages at our town hall. How perfect, I thought, and oh, how delicious being the only lesbian couple marching through those hallowed doors in our quaint little town populated by old Italians and Catholics. I could smell the fire and brimstone from my easy chair. So, as casually as I would've asked Diana if she felt like ordering in Chinese, I asked if she wanted to get a civil union. And just as casually, she said yes. I only wish I had remembered the old adage: you get what you pay for.

In the days leading up to our union, Diana seemed a little edgy and a lot less than enthusiastic, at one point calling the town hall to make sure that having our nuptials filmed by the local news wasn't a stipulation of the freebie deal. Imagine the explaining she'd have to do if, while eating dinner that night, her unwitting parents happened to look up from their pot roast and saw us getting hitched as they passed each other the potatoes and carrots. Yes, after fourteen years, Diana still referred to me as her "friend" to her parents. An only child, she hadn't the heart to disappoint them by revealing who she was and what we meant to each other, while I, another damaged product of a homophobic society, didn't know I had the right to protest this. But all that, of course, was of little importance because I had always had faith that she would eventually do the right thing. If my feelings weren't reason enough to inspire her, surely our civil union would be.

So on Valentine's Day, in our coordinating red and pink turtlenecks, flanked by a few close friends, we arrived for our date with the town's first female mayor and her staff of two young women, just as open-minded and progressive as she was. Unaccustomed to being open to anyone but our closest friends, we stood under the makeshift trellis of roses lost in the unreality of the scene, parroting the words and vows of love and lifelong commitment as the mayor recited them. After the mayor's secretary snapped a few photos with her digital camera, we all choked down some complimentary wedding cake and champagne and were off. Although I had always imagined the affair would feel more magical, all I focused on during the ride home was that we were now finally, truly committed. So what if we hadn't planned a honeymoon? So what if our families weren't there? We would have a fancy something or other in the summer and announce it to everyone then. I was satisfied with that as we continued our Wednesday-evening routine as though we had simply run an errand at Target. It was year fourteen of the relationship, and by then I was well acquainted with the art of self-delusion and the peacekeeping potential of low expectations.

As the weeks and months marched on, however, I wondered why things weren't better between Diana and me. I assumed the civil union would allay the angst and resentment I had been harbouring toward her for never acknowledging us to her family. It was a major step after all. It was on paper now, sealed by the town clerk and on file in the Vital Statistics Department just like a real marriage. But the summer came and went with no reception, no honeymoon, and a lot of simmering questions. In my haste to be part of the Valentine's Day wedding marathon and to secure our tenuous love, the one thing that hadn't occurred to me was that our relationship had already declined into an amiable roommate situation before we ever exchanged vows. Neither one of us, it seemed, least of all me, was willing or able to admit it.

One month before our first anniversary, Diana's fortieth birthday loomed, empowering her with both the will and ability to acknowledge that we weren't happy and hadn't been for a long time. This news was not shocking to me—so why was I so devastated when she said she was moving out? Maybe it was my classic Leo stubbornness or my general reluctance to concede defeat of any kind. I mean, legislators and activists had fought hard to make gay relationships legal and legitimate. Didn't we owe it to them to make our marriage work? Framing it in those terms helped me look myself in the mirror rather than have to admit the shock really came from a frantic fear of losing my safe, comfortable life.

For weeks I believed I was mourning the loss of Diana; she was my best friend and partner my entire adult life and the thought of living without her and starting over on my own was unbearable and terrifying. After a couple of desperate, maudlin attempts to change her mind, I realized the sobering truth that Diana had already arrived at the point of no return by the time she broached the subject. Even though couples therapy is sometimes just a last-ditch exercise in futility, at least it makes you feel better about a relationship's demise, like every effort had been exhausted before the curtain closed. I expected that chance—hell, I'd earned it living on the outskirts of her family for so many years, a second-class citizen in my own life. But Diana had already checked out and was merely awaiting the availability of her new apartment.

I flashed back to the starry night in 1993 on a secluded beach off Commercial Street in Provincetown, Massachusetts, when Diana got down in the sand on bended knee and asked me to marry her. It was romantic and clichéd in all the right ways, but it was also a time when marriage was only a pleasant abstract in gay people's minds. Too young and unwounded to be cynical, I said yes, believing her, believing in her. Now that we were going down, the least we could do was go down with a fight. But there would be no fight—just a separation that was as passionless as the last years of our relationship, just me watching as she awkwardly plotted her escape from our life.

The Script's "Breakeven" was on the charts then and the line "What am I supposed to do when I'm all choked up and you're okay"† was the soundtrack of my existence, a constant loop in my mind and on every radio station. Losing Diana was all I could see, feel, smell, and taste. I had allowed it to consume me. Force-feeding myself Nutri-Grain bars to stay alive, I'd weep down the quiet halls of the house before she came home from work until the day she drove away with her clothes and furniture packed in her car, leaving behind divots in the carpet and an emptiness that started growing in me like a cancer years before her departure.

How ironic and more than a little naive that after years of bitching about how the government had no right legislating our personal lives, I had pinned my hopes on a government decree to save my relationship. Although civil union legislation was a tremendous victory that opened the door to full marriage equality in my state, the breakdown of my marriage shows that when it comes to love, no law in the world has the power to make or break it. Ours had broken long before I began celebrating this political landmark, and as auspicious as it was, it couldn't mend the fractured pieces I clung to for so long.

Whether it was the officiousness and permanence of a legal document binding us in mediocrity forever or something else that became Diana's catalyst for change, it was a change we both needed. I was able to move on thanks to a counsellor who helped me overcome my anxiety, to friends old and new, and to the profound sense of relief and hopefulness I found learning that I could live happily on my own.

Now, as the debate for marriage equality in America rages on, I know the key to a happy and successful relationship is turned solely from within. Anti-gay politics and the intolerant opinions of others were excuses for my dissatisfaction; I'm the one who tolerated the consequences. It was a hard lesson to learn, but it's really about knowing what I need and deserve from a partner and, more importantly, recognizing when I'm not getting it.

JEAN COPELAND is a high school English teacher and writer from southern Connecticut. Her fiction and personal essays have appeared in sharkreef. org, *Connecticut Review*, *Texas Told'em*, *P.S. What I Didn't Say*, *Off the Rocks*, *Best Lesbian Love Stories*, *Harrington Lesbian Literary Quarterly*, *The First Line*, hotmetalpress.net, and prickofthespindle.com.

† The Script, "Breakeven," on *The Script*, Phonogenic Records, 2008, compact disc.

The Accidental Husband

MAX MOSHER

THEY SAY INDIA CHANGES you. Although I had backpacked through Europe, I had never been farther east than Istanbul. I prepared for culture shock and overwhelming poverty. Fortunately, I was going with my friend Dervla, a more experienced and fiercely independent traveller. She moved to England at eighteen while I went to university in exotic Guelph, Ontario. She attended teachers' college in Australia while I did my master's in my hometown of Toronto. She travelled the length of Africa largely on her own or with other young women. I lived abroad but in Dublin, Ireland. Friends since high school, we hoped touring India wouldn't tear us apart. We didn't expect to end up married.

We were the only North Americans in our tour group, which

consisted of Brits, Australians, and Kiwis. While travelling with a group of people in a foreign country, you quickly create your own micro-culture, despite your disparate backgrounds. Pushed out of your comfort zone, you experience so much each day that by dinnertime you long for the comforting familiarity of discussing TV shows over curry masala. It doesn't take many long train rides before you start acting like a family.

If we were a family, Liz and Phil were the cool grandparents. A white-haired British couple, they had married young and done well for themselves. Liz had always wanted to travel to India; Phil had not. Indeed, his job back home involved safety inspections. He was always the one to harangue cab drivers about using their cell phones. Despite their age, they were enthusiastic and genuinely enjoyed travelling with a group of mostly young people.

Playing the role of the kind of weird uncle you rarely see was Mike. A solitary older man from the north of England, he came to India to take interchangeable photographs of sunrises and sunsets. He kept to himself and hated the food, subsisting on plain rice and bananas. Consequently, he lost a lot of weight, to the point where we worried about him. He brushed it off, claiming he'd put it back on when he returned home to bangers and mash. This was his fourth trip to India.

Dervla and I were closest with the Aussies and Kiwis around our age, a hilarious couple named Ankit and Dani in particular. Ankit's parents were from India and he could speak Hindi, which he used to surprise locals when they tried to cut in line ahead of him. He had visited India a lot as a kid but was a proud New Zealander. He said he was touring India, instead of visiting family there, because he wanted to show his fiancée the country in a way that would be most fun for her before they got married. Ankit could always be trusted to have packed the best cookies for long bus rides.

Then there was Kathy, the rebellious little sister you have to worry about. At first, I thought this single girl from Australia was kind of fun. But issues arose pretty early in the trip. She drank every night, and when she got drunk she could be verbally abusive. She was also a bit too eager to take pictures of local children, touching and rearranging them to get the photo just right. Stuff like that bothered Dervla. "You would never do that to children back home," she'd say. Most problematic, she had a habit of befriending local men and disappearing for whole days or nights at a time. She missed our camel ride through the Thar Desert in order to go to a party with a group of men she had just met. When she rejoined us at the hotel, she barely spoke of it.

The person responsible for everything, from hailing eight auto rickshaws for us outside chaotic train stations to dealing with Phil not wanting to cover his head in a Sikh temple, was our tour leader, Kuldeep. Handsome and charming, he came from a surprisingly well-off family. In the beautiful city of Udaipur, he showed us an abandoned temple his family owned right on the lake. I have no idea why he was showing us around India.

Some people might be surprised that I'd choose this sort of trip, so let me explain. I see the same ads on Facebook that a lot of gay guys do—shirtless, happy body builders on "exclusively gay" cruises. First off, how cute that Facebook thinks I have the money for luxury cruises even after I listed my profession as writer. I understand why some people appreciate the comfort and sense of safety of an all-queer travel tour. It's liberating to feel like you won't confront homophobia, at least from your fellow travellers. And there's the increased possibility of a travel romance, although given my history with men, even with a tour group filled with gays, the only man I would end up taking to bed would be a paperback David Sedaris.

Even if I hadn't planned the trip with Dervla, it wouldn't have occurred to me to go with a gay tour. In my day-to-day life, friends and colleagues of different sexualities and backgrounds surround me. Why should travel be any different? I've been fortunate and haven't faced discrimination since I was in high school. Often, I forget I'm a minority until someone reminds me. When I meet a new person I don't so much come out of the closet as speak freely and openly. And I talk a lot. By the third *Sex and the City* reference, most people figure out I'm gay.

I know for some gay people their group of queer friends act as their "urban family," but I've been lucky to have a close, supportive relationship with my biological one. Other gay men have been the source of drama in my life far more than my parents ever were, even when I was a teenager. When I came out to them at fifteen, they acted like it was no big deal, despite my tearful hysterics. They had known for some time.

But they were a little worried about my grandmother, whom we call Granda due to my inability to pronounce "grandma" as a toddler. Born in 1921, Granda's life is typical of her generation. She worked as a secretary until the war ended. After that, her only careers were wife and mother in Kitchener, Ontario.

My grandfather had been a Red Tory back when those existed, but Granda has never cared much for politics — she believes in the Queen and finishing all the food on your plate. Nothing in her background prepared her for a queer grandson who liked Indian food. When I began dating my first boyfriend, James, my mom offered to tell her about me because we knew she'd figure it out eventually.

Mom said Granda was surprised, but she'd never want to say or do anything that hurt my feelings or caused a familial rift. Sometime later, I was given a better insight into her feelings when my old friend Laura, who treats Granda like she's her own grandmother, told me they had discussed it. According to her, my grandmother said, "To tell you the truth, when I found out Max was gay I was a little uncomfortable. But James is a lovely young man, and he makes Max happy. And that's what's important."

"Should I have told you that?" Laura asked nervously.

"I am so glad you told me that!" I answered.

I have been fortunate. Throughout my life, even people unaccustomed to homosexuality have accepted me because they liked and supported me. Liz and Phil wouldn't have known any out gay people when they were younger, but they readily accepted me and my high-camp sense of humour. To this day, Liz, like a real relative, follows all my posts on Facebook. The nonchalance with which both my tour group and my grandmother accepted me was a lesson in the importance of coming out — once most people know you as a person, being gay is just another aspect of your personality.

In India, I never felt like I was the odd one in the group.

Okay, there was one exception. One day during a train ride, Ankit told a story about getting a colonoscopy, but he made eye contact with me at exactly the wrong moment. "So I'm lying there, ass up, and the doctor's about to stick it in. And, y'know, it's the most uncomfortable . . ." He looked at me. "Well, not uncomfortable, but for a man, it's the worst . . . um, for *most* men, it's the worst feeling . . ." I kept staring at him, with a wry smile on my face. "Oh, God," he sighed, giving up the anecdote. Everyone laughed.

While the group understood the nature of our relationship, at least initially Kuldeep thought Dervla and I were a couple. Unlike Emma and Nick, a straight girl and guy from New Zealand who were travelling together as friends and always requested separate beds, Dervla and I were fine with bunking together and were often given what we liked to call the honeymoon suites: in romantic Udaipur, we had a window seat and stained glass; in yellow-bricked Jaisalmer, we looked out the window of our personal sitting room at an expansive view of the surrounding desert stretching to the Pakistan border.

Eventually, Kuldeep must have figured it out. In Pushkar, a pilgrimage site for Hindus and home to a lake said to have grown from Lord Shiva's tears, our hotel had a TV and DVD player. Instead of a historical epic, I suggested the group watch *Dostana*, a Bollywood comedy about two men who pretend to be gay to live with a beautiful woman. It is not a good movie, but I zealously pushed everyone to watch it like I was planning a pride parade.

Kuldeep wasn't the only one confused about our relationship. Unfamiliar with the gay guy–straight girl dynamic, I think most Indians saw us as a young couple, a misconception strengthened by our physical comfort with each other. Linking arms on rickety rickshaws may have looked romantic, but we were really holding on for dear life to avoid face-planting onto the road.

Having never travelled with a man before, Dervla noted other advantages. When ducking out of the hotel by herself, she saw men staring at her. Even in places used to tourists, a young, white woman on her own aroused attention. People would often try to talk to her, either to get her into a shop or to engage her in a conversation as rambling as the labyrinthine streets themselves. While wanting to be respectful (Dervla made sure her shoulders were always covered, unlike some Western tourists who dress not so much for India as for Laguna Beach), she bristled at being treated so blatantly as an object of curiosity.

Going out accompanied by me was completely different. Attempts to engage her in conversation decreased, as did the staring. My presence acted like the fake wedding ring single female travellers often slip on to ward off unwanted attention. At some point I learned if I made eye contact with a man who was staring at Dervla, he would quickly avert his eyes. I had discovered the non-verbal way of saying, "Stop coveting my property!"

I had a beard (because I didn't want to shave regularly) and began dropping my voice when speaking to peddlers. "Leave us alone!" I practically shouted at a would-be holy man in Varanasi who persistently tried to sell us flowers. When a pack of barking dogs surrounded us in the Portuguese-flavoured town of Panijim, I stepped in front of Dervla and began yelling, "No! Down!" (In English, of course.)

I am not a tall man, and back home on the sidewalks of Toronto pedestrians find it easy to ignore me or walk right into me, assuming I will be the one to move out of the way first. "Excuse me!" I sometimes feel like yelling. "You can't walk through me. I, too, am made of matter!" But in India, I never felt ignored. It was nice to feel like I could protect myself and Dervla, even if it was just brash bravado. Although it made my feminist soul guilty, I discovered the fun of the masculine protector role.

Dervla's feelings, on the other hand, were mixed. "It was liberating and felt much safer travelling with a guy," she later told me. "But also frustrating. I shouldn't have to feel like I need to rely on a man for protection." When travelling in Africa on her own, she had garnered attention but felt more comfortable speaking up and asserting herself. But in India she felt either on display or, if accompanied by me, ignored.

"Also," she added, lowering her voice. "I don't want this to come out the wrong way, but I couldn't help but think, If only they knew you were gay . . ." I hadn't realized that, while my beard and I were a beard for Dervla (disguising her as a married woman), she was simultaneously a beard for me, helping me pass as straight in a conservative, religious country.

I began to understand how difficult it was for the women on our tour of the Hawa Mahal, a former palace built in the last year of the eighteenth century in the pink-painted Jaipur. It's notable for its honeycomb-inspired windows from which the ladies of the Maharaja's court looked down upon the street. As followers of the strict rules of *purdah* (face-covering), the women could only observe the everyday life of the city through intricate, lattice-worked peepholes.

The Hawa Mahal is a popular site for Indian tourists. Unfortunately, many of the visitors there that hot, humid day were less interested in snapping pictures of the gorgeous architecture than of the women of our tour. I heard stories of young men blatantly pointing at Dervla and the others and shoving cameras right in their faces. One girl in our group, while resting in the shade, covered her head with a sweater, enforcing her own *purdah* technique. How sad that in a palace designed to shield women from prying eyes, modern-day women still felt the need to hide.

Photographers were also a nuisance at the Taj Mahal. The building itself lives up to expectations, though I will let you in on a secret: because they ask you to take off your shoes, the inside smells like feet. Some Indian tourists wanted pictures with white tourists (female and blond, preferably). It was cute sometimes, as when the request came from a group of giggling schoolgirls. It was less so when it came from grown men. One in particular approached me asking something I didn't understand. I first thought he wanted me to take a picture of him. Then I realized he wanted a photo with Dervla and was asking my permission. On principle, as well as knowing that Dervla wouldn't want to, I said no. The man pleaded with me. "Well, now you're getting me annoyed!" I snapped, in a voice not my own. The man sulked away while I realized I didn't particularly like being this male protector who so easily raised his voice at strangers.

The naive traveller thinks you travel to learn about other places; the experienced one knows you learn about yourself. When we compare ourselves to characters in movies, Dervla says I'm like the cliché gay best friend, always ready with dating advice and a sassy comeback. But in India I played a very different role, that of the protective hetero husband. I call it a role, but it didn't feel like I was being phony at the time. Rather, the circumstances brought out a long-dormant part of my personality, one I rarely need in Toronto where the only one I need to protect is myself.

We all have different roles we play. They can appear when travelling to far-flung locations or when we're at home with people we've known all our lives. I didn't know I could act like a hetero husband until travelling with Dervla encouraged it, just like my grandmother, in her eighties at the time, didn't know she could accept homosexuality until she found out she had a gay grandson. We try on different hats for those we love. It's what families do.

My brief stint as a heterosexual husband was interesting, but once I returned I packed it away with my backpack. Like the red, baggy Aladdin pants I wore camel riding, it was fun at the time, but it's just not me.

MAX MOSHER is a freelance writer who lives in Toronto. He wrote and edited for *WORN Fashion Journal* and wrote a style column for the *Toronto Standard*. His work has been published in the *Utne Reader*. You can follow him on Twitter at @max_mosher_.

What She Taught Me

ELLEN RUSSELL

ONE OF THE GOOD things about cancer, said someone in the grief support group, is the opportunity to know how much you are loved before you die. I nodded along with all of the other widows. They were grandmothers from the most conventional corners of Heterosexual Land, and their families didn't look much like my own. But that observation clearly spoke to all of us widows. Kate's parting gift was her talent for connecting with people, and those loving connections enveloped us both as she faced her death.

Kate knew a little something about reaching out to people to spin a web of love around herself. And around me. Kate's idea of bliss was to find herself in a puppy pile of warm human connection. She "went after people," as she liked to say. With her genius for nuzzling her way into people's hearts, she was continuously creating family for herself and for me. As my grieving evolves and I am able to treasure the good things, she continues to teach me how to reach past difficulties and embrace people. It doesn't come as naturally to me as it did to Kate, but it's an art that I'm trying to practise.

We met at a friend's birthday brunch in Toronto many years ago, when she and I were both twenty-six. Initially, I wasn't sure what to make of this goofy, playful tomboy. It was her supermodel routine that clinched it for me. After brunch, I tagged along as the gang went off to play co-ed baseball. For me, the game was unbearably tense. But then I watched as Kate worked her magic.

The guys on the team were very competitive, and they were increasingly impatient with the women, who were mostly their girlfriends. The women became less and less confident as their boyfriends got more and more irritable. But Kate was nobody's girlfriend. She had the ambiguous privilege of being sought after in the co-ed league. In the most revealing of gendered insults masquerading as compliments, she was deemed to be a woman who could "really" play baseball.

As the gender tension escalated, Kate did one of her goofball interventions. She made what I assume was a good play, then took off her baseball glove and put it on her head. She started strutting supermodel-style: swivelling her hips and yukking it up about ruining her new hairdo or breaking a nail. The women seemed delighted that Kate was using gender stereotypes to mock gender stereotypes, and the playful spectacle was so lacking in hostility that the men were unable to resist either. I was smitten. I had never seen someone blend good-natured satire and politically astute improvisation. Thanks to her goofy brand of activism, people emerged from the encounter seeming more connected to one another.

For almost twenty years, Kate gently showed me how to reach out and connect. I live a lot in my head, but I have a deep political commitment to the importance of community—I just don't always know what to do about it. Kate persistently encouraged me to walk the talk: go after people you want to connect to, name the tensions that inevitably bubble up, and search for a lighthearted, loving way to transcend those tensions to get to the human connection we all crave. Be brave and don't let the eruption of sexism, homophobia, or anything else hold you back. You will screw up and that is okay; you'll manage. Just don't miss the opportunity. It's a lesson I'm still trying to learn.

Kate really wanted to *know* people. She wasn't content with the superficial interactions we routinely have with neighbours and co-workers (although within a week of moving to a new place, she'd be well on her way to knowing the names of all the children and dogs on the street). She wanted real closeness. She would sit down with a friend and dispense with the mundane pleasantries by cutting to the chase: "Tell me something that you really want me to know about how your life is these days," she'd say.

It was remarkable to see people blossom in the presence of someone who focused that sort of attention on the desire to connect. She paid exquisite attention to respecting and supporting children, and her relationship with our nieces and nephews still continues to remind me of the power of her love. As our nephew Christopher Reynolds wrote a few days before her death:

Aunt Kate,

When I was just a little boy I came to Toronto and visited you and Ellen. At the time my world was chaotic and I felt small; in fact, I WAS small. Then you invited me to sit at your dining room table to share a meal and some chocolate almond bark. I was maybe 7 or 8 at the time, but we talked about politics, social issues and our feelings, and you helped me to understand what it was like to be different and made me realize that not only is that an okay thing, but that it can be a beautiful thing. Most amazingly, as we sat on either end of that big table, you didn't talk AT me even once—you talked with me—and you were, I'm sure of it, the very first adult to do that with me. The very first adult to offer me the space and the dignity I needed to express myself. This had, and has had, a tremendous effect on my life. You empowered me by validating my young mind, giving me license to have an opinion, no matter how immature and malformed it might have been.

I often think about that meal we shared, that beautiful, respectful, perfect meal, and I will always remember it as one of my most formative experiences and I am giddy with the thought of one day giving that same space to a young voice in my home one day, Kate-style. I love you very, very much and I can't wait to teach the world what you taught me.

Kate's gentle insistence on deepening connection built a family around us in a way I'd never imagined. Growing up, I'd understood family to be a strictly biological concept. For Kate, family was something much more. Sure, she had buckets of wonderful brothers and sisters and a big, extended Catholic family from the Maritimes. But even that sprawling family included, without a doubt, friends and neighbours who had supported Kate's mom when she lost her husband. Christmas morning in the Reynolds house involved running around the neighbourhood in pyjamas to visit of all the nearest and dearest. This template for what a family could be, along with her desire to really know people, inspired Kate's quest to have lots of loving connections.

Because of Kate, I came to see family as an evolving, fluid entity that requires attentive nurturing. It's made of some people you share DNA with and some you don't. At times, we lose people we consider to be family. People sometimes evolve in ways that don't fit together so well, and old traumas can make it difficult to sustain the safety that connection requires. Those losses are never taken lightly; they are always mourned. But there is never love without loss. Families are never static.

Before Kate got sick, I didn't really grasp the depth of the community, the family, that she had created. In 2008, Kate was diagnosed right off the bat with stage IV colon cancer, so the prognosis was never good. I remember trembling at her first articulate statement as she left the doctor's office. "But," she said in shock, "I'm supposed to grow old with you." We went home to make phone calls. One by one, she needed to tell all of the people she loved. For hours it went on, the crying and the phone calls.

Around us mobilized an incredible network of so many loving people. It is impossible to convey how this community enveloped us. I would have lost my mind if I didn't have so many arms to tumble into. Folks took on countless tasks to keep us functioning. Of course, Kate saw this parade of activity as an opportunity to socialize. Every two weeks, Joanne would sit with her at the hospital when her chemotherapy marathon got started, and they would do their best to say everything that needed saying before the treatments eventually prevented Kate from focusing on conversation. Meanwhile, I would do errands, Peggy would shop, Alison handled the paperwork, and heaven knows what other needs were addressed as Diana and Doris coordinated a large network of people who sprung into action. All would be made ready for the two days of home-administered portion of her chemo that kept us housebound for more like a week. And then the phone calls would start, as Irene and Wendy and Kate's siblings kept vigil over Kate's struggles with chemo.

After Kate's death, Joanne related an incident that speaks to me over my shoulder as I write this. Joanne glimpsed someone across the oncology waiting room that she knew. She mentioned to Kate that she liked this person, but they had fallen out of touch. Joanne may even have said that she didn't want to intrude on her friend. Kate roused herself at this comment. "You have been given an opportunity," Kate told her. "Go and speak to your friend. You cannot squander this chance to make you both happier."

Kate fought hard to grasp her own opportunity, and after twenty rounds of chemo there was a glimmer of hope. She decided to go to Montreal for a risky surgery, and Kate's dear friend Brenda and I mobilized to make it happen. The ten days in Montreal turned into four months as the surgery backfired and Kate lost ground day by day. Through those long months, countless people from all over the country came to stay with us. Almost every afternoon, Kate hung out with a sister, brother, or friend who had flown in from who-knows-where. Those precious visits were a continuous testament to the many loves in Kate's life. It was a delight to see her energy rally when she anticipated the next visit from one of her vast family.

In the hospital, Kate was the belle of the ball. People she knew for only the last months of her life also became family after a fashion. She wanted to know all the nurses in the same deep way she wanted to know everyone, asking about their kids and the challenges of their shifts. Medical and custodial staff would stop by the room before they went on shift or hang out afterward if they hadn't gotten a chance to check in with Kate. Sometimes I would get a bit antsy, fearing that Kate wouldn't rest for all of the people coming and going. But it did so feed her soul to reach out.

On Halloween, Kate prowled the surgery ward with Brenda and me (and her IV pole) as she gave everyone candy from a plastic orange pumpkin. For Christmas, we got her a blow-up reindeer for her wall, and I'm told it still graces the family room at the hospital. "Greg," a teenaged liver transplant recipient farther down the hall, became close with Kate. He came to wish her a happy New Year in his bedpan hat and impressively decorated walker.

Just weeks before she died, Kate marshalled her fleeting energy to reach out to Greg. Once he was stable enough to transfer back to his home province, he became distraught. After a couple of years spent mostly in hospitals, leaving the family he had created in the surgery ward thrust him into the unknown. At one point, a nurse came to Kate, saying the Greg was throwing everyone out of his room and refusing food. Would Kate come to talk to him? Kate listened gently as he spoke of his fears and the incalculable distance between himself and the world of healthy seventeen-year-olds. She didn't try to cheer him up with platitudes — she just listened and cared and affirmed all his courage and resourcefulness that would serve him so well. As she left his room, she was pleased that she could use her gifts when it mattered so much. I recall bursting with love for her as she shuffled back to her room exhausted. She and I both knew on some level that we were heading toward a future that would not include her discharge from the hospital.

Now that Kate has gone, she is still teaching me how to reach past adversity to have love and joy in my life, despite the grief. I'm astonished to find that I can keep loving Kate deeply and reach out to my new love, Hilary. She is another widow who lost her long-term partner, Kathryn, to cancer. I guess you could call what we are creating a blended family. Her history with her partner and mine with Kate have melded into a new present and an unknown future. It's certainly unfamiliar and maybe unorthodox, but reaching for people across previously unthinkable boundaries is just what Kate showed me how to do. So, my family is morphing too. However you might define it, my family now includes Kate's family and Hilary's family and Kathryn's family.

When I recently moved into my new house, a work party

got organized. Not to be left out, Kathryn's eighty-five-year-old father, Jack, wanted to chip in. I could try to translate my relationship to Jack into conventional terms, but the old words used to describe family just get too cumbersome (my father-in-law from my new partner's previous relationship, perhaps?). But why bother? As Kate might say, life is short and you should take any opportunity to connect when you can. So if Jack wants to join in supporting his deceased daughter's partner's new girlfriend, then that loving impulse is plenty for me. Kate was all about nudging me to reach out and connect, so why wouldn't I open my arms wide?

ELLEN RUSSELL is an assistant professor in the digital media and journalism program at Wilfrid Laurier University. She usually focuses on political economy and has published articles and a book on financial regulation and Canadian political economy. Her work has been published in many magazines and newspapers, including the *Toronto Star*, the *Globe and Mail*, rabble.ca, and *This Magazine*. She was previously a senior economist at the Canadian Centre for Policy Alternatives.

Hiddur Mitzvah[†]

S. BEAR BERGMAN

ON FRIDAYS, FOR SHABBOS, we bring out the Shabbos things, the items made beautiful by custom and law — *hiddur mitzvah* is the term for this, the enhancing of a good deed by making the objects used in it beautiful as a way to sanctify the act and praise HaShem who commanded it. In our house, as in many houses with multiple generations of Jews and Jewish relatives, the objects are . . . well. *Hodge-podge* would be a kind term.

We have two *challah* covers, one that my husband, Ishai, was given as a gift upon the occasion of his conversion to Judaism and one that my mother needlepointed for me when she was going through her needlework phase because no one wanted a new *tallit*. Our Shabbos candlesticks are battered and brass, a set I must have purchased at some stage and have used off and on for twenty years, reluctant to buy myself a set when I know that both of my grandmothers, still living, have beautiful ones that I will want to use when the time comes. These, in the meantime, have a somewhat utilitarian nature, but they're familiar and therefore comforting. Our Kiddush cup belonged to my Nana Janie, my great-grandmother in my maternal line, and if you've never had the experience of watching your toddler son wrap his chubby little baby paws around the silver cup his great-great-grandmother got as a wedding present and take a baby sip of Shabbos wine, I'll just say: It's pretty great.

We try to always have guests for Shabbos dinner on a Friday night. We don't always manage to get to *shul* on a Saturday morning because Saturday mornings are also gay dad's day at the local queer centre on the first Saturday and queer parents' mixer on the fourth Saturday, and this is also part of the deal. We want to make sure, for good and all, that our son, Stanley, knows plenty of other kids with queer parents and as many other kids with two trans dads as we can manage — not easy but not impossible. And at the same time, I grew up in a synagogue and all the grown-ups had known me forever, and my memories of Kiddush and laughter and making holidays with the same people my entire life are so rich, and so present, and kept me so connected to my congregation — and to my Jewish identity — even when forces of queerness started to seem like they might push me further away. The Sosteks, the Friedlanders, the Weisses, the Fischlers, the Arbeits: they welcomed baby-queer-me with tenderness and ran interference with my parents about it for, oh, a decade. Ish.

But Friday nights, we get the job done. Dinner, *challah*

from Harbord Bakery, which they keep for us now in a paper bag marked Bergman to make sure we always get one. I am not always the one to pick it up, but Ishai, whose last name is Wallace, decided we would get on the list faster with a more recognizably Jewish surname. I light candles and we make scooping motions with our hands and pour the Shabbos light over our son and, if they're into it, our guests. We pour a Kiddush cup of wine and share it, we all touch the bread and make a *motzi*, the blessing over bread, and then Ishai and I feed each other the first morsel, which still feels really, really nice. The candlelight does what candlelight is supposed to do, especially when combined with wine. We're all lovely and peaceful, even when the little dude starts campaigning for ice cream ten seconds after dinner has started.

He gets ice cream on Shabbos, that's what he remembers. After candles and wine, then there's ice cream. So, where is it?

And we invite people to share. Our kitchen table seats six, and we can—with judicious use of stools—expand to eight. We try to make a mix—some people with whom we've shared a lot of Shabbos, and some who are new friends. It takes a certain level of tolerance to come to dinner at our house, since the hosts disappear in turn after dinner to bathe the toddler and put him to bed, and often there is a command performance of story reading in the middle there. Stanley does not like to feel left out.

It's the way of having kids that religious observances tend to centre on them for a while when they're little. You can only do as much as the kid will sit through. That's all. So bringing friends and family to share Shabbos dinner is a way to both make sure we get to see them since we now go to bed at ten most nights and make sure that Stanley never remembers not knowing them. To make sure they feel like *family*, like *mishpokhe*, his Auntie Abi and his Sparkle Chris and his Tante Hanne and Uncle Zev and his Uncles Nik and Syrus and little cousin Amelie, their brand-new baby daughter. To whom he is not, in any sense, related, except that, of course and absolutely, these people are family.

I might have been older than Stanley when I first discovered that you could use those kinds of words—words that are heavy with default meanings, words that everyone understands—to make space for relationships that not everybody would understand. My son has got a couple of cousins like this, including Morgan, the teenager whom I usually shorthand to "my niece," even though the actual explanation has no siblings in it whatsoever. Ishai, my husband, refers to her as "the household teenager," Stanley talks about her as his cousin, and she refers to us as "her other parents" in some situations and "her uncles" in others. I think of them as words that already have so much meaning they won't mind, or maybe notice, if we slip our meaning in there as well. People don't ask her, they just assume, oh, your uncle, brother of your mother or father. No one jumps straight to "Oh, your uncle, husband of your parents' former live-in lover."

Now we have this kid of our own, a kid whose family tree is practically bent double with relatives of assorted kinds—blood, marriage, wine, and glitter—my parents' closest friends, our closest friends, legitimate blood relations, and people who declared upon Stanley's arrival in the world their intention to be his family. The person whose proper title, if we were being literal about this sort of a thing, is "person with whom Papa has had the longest and most tumultuous love affair and working relationship of his life" has claimed for herself the title "Fairy Godsmother." Okay, fair enough. Come for Shabbos, next time you're in town.

(She does.)

I could grade and assign distinctions, to be sure. In town, out of town, related by blood or marriage, wine or glitter, but I don't for two reasons: one, too many people are in more than one category, and two, where's the fun in that? Part of what I adore about the family that has coalesced around our Shabbos table and around our son is how magnificently diverse it is, in every way, how many genders and sensibilities and gets of interests and politics and points of view it contains, how many tattoos and how many piercings, how many racial and ethnic and religious combinations. I also adore how very befuddled my parents are by the recognition that, if their grandson is related to this mélange of people, then there is some way—however small—in which they are related to the lot of them too. Heh.

When Stanley was born, his Tante Hanne—my dear friend and collaborator, who has no children—sent Stanley her childhood baby blanket and her father's old cloth picture books from childhood. They're marvellous—the blanket is made of a pure white wool, spun soft, with the edges hand-bound for a long life. It was made for Hanne upon the occasion of her birth by her own great-grandmother and passed to Stanley through his non-traditional family ties. His Fairy Godsmother Kate, who has never met her own grandchildren because she is estranged from her only child, carries photos and videos of Stanley on her phone and shows them off as much as I do—okay, well, almost as much. His Grandspuncle and Grandsparkle—the parents of his Spuncle Jacob, obviously—*kvell* over his every milestone with obvious delight and forward the emails and photos of him I send to a truly astonishingly large group of people. They seem to have no concern about explaining that their son, the hetero-flexible rabbi, has made a kind of queer family with two transguys via both intention and sperm, and is now known to a rambunctious three-year-old as Spuncle Jacob.

Spuncle, by the way, is the portmanteau word made of *sperm* and *uncle* that our very earnest lesbian friends—one of whom is my husband's oldest friend in the world—made up. They do not appear to notice that the word *spunk* also appears in this word, and it is therefore a little giggle-worthy to the gay boys. Their two kids, whom we will become guardian to if, G-d forbid, anything were to happen to them, are some more of Stanley's cousins of no consanguinity whatsoever. It's their son Eli who, in his retelling of the Nativity story, relates that "Mary wanted to have a baby, so she asked her friends for a cup of sperm," because in his world, that's how babies are made. Hard to argue.

The world around Stanley is even more robust than he knows because he's still little and the people come around one or two or a dozen at a time. He's never been able to play with all his cousins at once. He has no idea how deep he is in *mishpokhe*, how many people claim him as their own.

This is exactly what I want for him. We fly places and Skype with people and do all manner of things to keep him connected and deepen the connections that exist, making Shabbos even when we're exhausted because it's where these things happen. Where the same faces appear over and over, where new friends and new jokes and new stories come to the table, where the old things get pulled out and polished and used with a certain mixture of reverence and work-a-day trust in their abilities, where every object and person and relationship has a story—where it came from, how we met it, what we thought at first, what we understand to be true now.

We tell and retell the stories so he will have heard them a million times before he's old enough to retell them once, and so he understands how much the story of a person or a thing can add to the enjoyment of them, and maybe most so that we can pull them out and polish them as well, tighten them up as storytellers will always and instinctively do with jokes or stories each time they tell them: make them a little better. Make them a little more beautiful with each retelling, fulfilling the obligation of *hiddur mitzvah*: making each story beautiful, in praise to HaShem, who has blessed us a million times with the winding of our stories together.

S. BEAR BERGMAN is an author, storyteller, and educator working to create positive, celebratory representations of trans lives who lives in Toronto. Recent or current projects include two fabulous children's storybooks featuring trans-identified kid characters, a performance about loving and living in a queer/ed Jewish family titled *Machatunim*, teaching pleasure-positive trans/gender-queer sex ed, and his sixth book, *Blood, Marriage, Wine & Glitter* (Arsenal Pulp, 2013). A longtime activist, Bear continues to work at the points of intersection between and among gender, sexuality, and culture, and spends a lot of time trying to discourage people from installing traffic signals there. Follow him online at sbearbergman.com.

† "Hiddur Mitzvah" first appeared in *Blood, Marriage, Wine & Glitter* (Arsenal Pulp Press, 2013).

Acknowledgments

MY DEEPEST THANKS TO the contributors to this collection who bravely shared such personal and heartfelt stories; this book would not exist without their hard work. I'd also like to thank the Faculty of Liberal Arts at Wilfrid Laurier University's Brantford campus and my colleagues there for their support of this project. I'd be remiss if I didn't thank Ruth Linka, Pat Touchie, and the dedicated team at TouchWood Editions for the continued support of personal essay anthologies and in exploring the changing nature of the family in the twenty-first century. I'd also like to thank my friend and mentor Lynne Van Luven, who set me on this track many years ago. If I am able to inspire even a fraction of the many students and young writers she has, I shall consider myself fortunate.

A SERIES OF ANTHOLOGIES ABOUT THE TWENTY-FIRST-CENTURY FAMILY

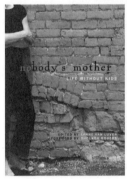
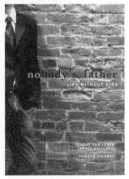

A Family by Any Other Name, How to Expect What You're Not Expecting, Somebody's Child, Nobody's Mother, and *Nobody's Father* are essay collections that explore queer relationships, childbirth, childlessness, and adoption. Together, these five books re-examine traditional definitions of parenthood and family.